KITCHEN&BATH
SHOWCASE™

Vitae Publishing, Inc.
Grand Rapids, MI

Published in the United States
by Vitae Publishing, Inc.
50 Monroe Avenue NW
Suite 400
Grand Rapids, MI 49503
1-800-284-8232

Library of Congress
Cataloging-in-Publication Data

Kitchen & Bath Showcase™
p. cm.
Includes indexes.
ISBN 1-883065-03-8 (hard)
      1-883065-04-6 (soft)
1. Kitchens – Design. 2. Bathrooms – Design. 3. Interior Decoration. 4. Cookery.
I. Kitchen & Bath Showcase

TX653.K52 1995 643'.4 - - dc20 94-38067 CIP

Vitae Publishing, Inc.

Chairman - John C. Aves
President - James C. Markle
Vice President - Gregory J. Dekker

Kitchen & Bath Showcase

Contributing Author - Ellen Cheever, CKD, CBD, ASID

Communication Manager - Christine H. Hoek
Production Manager - Douglas Koster
Production Designer - Kurt Dietsch
Production Artist - Mark Blodger
Copy Editor - David Knoor
Financial Management - Jeanne Seaman and Kathleen Kelly

Regional Editors

Gloria Blake, PhD
Maria Cutler
Anne K. Donahue
Betty Ereckson
Ron Frey
Gita Gidwani
Majda Kallab
Herb Motley
Marc Neid
Logan Pitts
Francine E. Port
Patty Stevens

Printed in Singapore
Typeset in USA by Vitae Publishing, Inc.

bulthaup (LA) Inc: The open kitchen and living space has become part of the lifestyle of the '90s. This clean, timeless design combines the practicality of white laminate with the warmth of natural wood. It's arranged with each function in mind, from closed storage for dry goods to glass cabinets for china and stemware. Stainless steel is used below the cooking area due to its ability to repel oil and grease.

◄

PROLOGUE

As you enter our kitchen, you begin a journey back in time.

Yes, ovens used to look like that. No, that's called linoleum. Isn't it lovely? Notice the lone two-prong electrical outlet there behind the coffee maker, microwave, toaster oven and food processor. Isn't it quaint? Yes, I agree; it is an odd place for a door. We've learned to warn each other with a yell before we come in. Oh, the candles? Well, they serve a dual purpose – more light and a little ambiance.

Things will look very different in the kitchen we're building. It will work for *us*. It will be a large, open gathering place with lots of light – the family's crossroads for socializing, food preparation and meals.

Our designer is asking great questions. "How are you planning to entertain? Where do you want to stand to see the gardens? Where do you usually enter the house? How do you plan to use counter space?" Our four-year-old wants a bigger refrigerator door so we can display more of his paintings.

With the help of our thought-provoking designer, we made the necessary design decisions. He is saving us money as well as mistakes and headaches. But the process of finding him in the first place would have been a lot easier if we had been able to use this beautiful book as a resource.

The top designers in the world are featured here, along with gorgeous photography of their kitchen and bath designs. The perfect designer and lots of ideas are right here for anyone planning to build or remodel a kitchen or bath. This book is definitely the place to start your search for a design professional.

Gregory J. Dekker, IFDA
Vitae Publishing

TABLE OF CONTENTS

Showcase of Kitchen and Bath Design

by Ellen Cheever,
CKD, CBD, ASID

The kitchen. No other room in the home has changed more. Once women couldn't wait to get out of the kitchen. Today, it's often the favorite gathering and socializing space for the entire family. The kitchen has become the "living room" of the American home.

Early in this century, kitchens were associated with grease, grime, and drudgery. Strictly utilitarian, kitchens were separate spaces – walled-off rooms usually hidden in the back of the house. In the 1940s and '50s, kitchens may have received a face-lift, but they remained the realm of the full-time homemaker who made dinner (usually meat and potatoes) every night and served it to a waiting family. Entertaining centered around special holidays or family dinners on Sunday. The kids' kitchen activity often was limited to dish duty. And "real men" didn't cook except for an occasional performance at the barbecue grill.

Changes and Challenges

During the last three decades, our society has seen dramatic shifts in traditional family roles and lifestyles. We also have witnessed an explosion of new technology – introducing everything from microwave cooking to computerized recipe storage – which has changed the way we live. These changes have been identified through several major research projects conducted by the National Kitchen and Bath Association and the University of Illinois Small Homes Council. Such research has led to an entire new set of planning standards adopted by both the academic community and by practicing design professionals.

The evolution of new planning standards is the result of how we live now. Today's kitchen plan must meet the room's new demands as a multi-purpose gathering space that is attractive and comfortable, and still fulfill its main role as a highly functional area for food preparation and storage. According to a study

Kitchen Classics, Inc.:
The reflective luster of vivid
cabinetry and the generous use
of tile join forces to create a
distinctly personal space.
▲

conducted at the University of Minnesota for the National Kitchen and Bath Association, there is more than one person in the typical kitchen about 69% of the time. It's clear that the kitchen is no longer a one-woman sweat box. Rather, it has become a space where the family comes together to share in meal planning, preparation and cleanup.

In addition to food preparation, the kitchen is now the scene of many non-cooking activities such as doing homework, paying bills, socializing, even watching TV. It's a room where comfortable seating and gathering space for non-cooks must be planned, and where work centers must accommodate the second or third cook who's inspired to chop, baste, bake and sauté.

DISCOVERY, DEFINITION AND DESIGN

In today's kitchen, both women and men are discovering the joy of cooking! For many people, cooking has become a hobby – a form of relaxation in our fast-paced world. To others, it is simply one more task in a busy day – to be done efficiently and well. In either case, to be most effective, the setting of this activity must be designed to reflect the personal style of the cook(s) and the preferences of the family.

As societal barriers that once defined who spent time in the kitchen crumbled, the walls sequestering the space were removed in favor of an open relationship with other rooms of the house. The kitchen may be adjacent to the breakfast nook, dining room, or family room – the popular "great room" concept. Increased traffic and visual exposure from other areas present special considerations during the planning process, such as the need for quiet appliances, a flexible lighting system, and an efficient ventilation system capable of quickly removing airborne grease and smoke contaminates.

The enhanced status of the kitchen is reflected in its overall emphasis on style. This is especially evident in the cabinetry. As it is often viewed from other more formal areas of the home, better kitchen cabinetry is expected to have a fine furniture look, while maintaining the durable qualities of kitchen cabinetry. Exquisite cabinet finishes, heavily detailed moldings, wood-trimmed counter sections, hardwood

Ellen Cheever, Heritage Custom Kitchens: Classic white cabinets, combined with an antique baker's table, create a traditional kitchen. Built-in appliances are paneled to match the cabinetry. Solid-surface counter, with an integral sink, provide functional worktops.

▲

floors, and appliances virtually hidden by panels matching the cabinetry are just some of the design choices available to help create a kitchen which looks like an extension of the living room.

The kitchen today has doubled its average number of appliances from three to six, and typically includes a refrigerator, cooktop with hood, conventional oven, microwave, dishwasher, and sink with food waste disposal. Finding space for these appliances is a challenge; their arrangement and configuration has affected the traditional "work triangle" concept. The triangle still works, it has just changed shape! For example, a design may incorporate two overlapping triangles, or it might replace the three-pointed shape with a square. Regardless of the number of appliances, providing an efficient work flow with minimal steps and adequate counterspace close to all appliances remains critical to a good kitchen plan.

Because the sink does double duty – serving the cook during both food preparation and cleanup – it is the most frequently used appliance in the kitchen. Actually considered a water appliance, the primary sink is located near the dishwasher and recycling area.

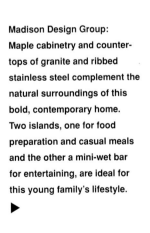

Madison Design Group: Maple cabinetry and countertops of granite and ribbed stainless steel complement the natural surroundings of this bold, contemporary home. Two islands, one for food preparation and casual meals and the other a mini-wet bar for entertaining, are ideal for this young family's lifestyle.

▶

A growing trend is a kitchen featuring two sinks. In such cases, the second sink is usually used for food preparation tasks and is best placed adjacent to the refrigerator or cooktop.

Changes in the American diet have had a significant impact on design. A lighter, fresher style of cooking has replaced the heavy cooking of yesteryear. Today's cook often shops for fresh food on the weekend and prepares a gourmet feast as a highlight. During the week, cooking may be limited to reheats from the weekend's feast, warm-ups from take-out establishments, or other quick and easy alternatives to an elaborate, multi-course meal. This lifestyle shift translates into a need for less storage space for food stuffs and ingredients, but more storage for microwave-safe dishes, containers for leftovers or individual portions, and a selection of plastic bags for storage and freezer use.

The typical family stores approximately twice as many pieces of equipment as a post-World War II family did. Consider some of the modern options in small appliances alone: food processors, blenders, juicers, pasta machines, deep fryers, woks, toaster ovens, coffee makers, and coffee bean grinders all require accessible storage space. It is also common today for a family to have an extensive collection of tableware – several sets of dishes, a variety of serving pieces, and special holiday dinnerware. The well-equipped kitchen may also house an impressive personal library of cookbooks. These kitchens require a well-engineered storage system – a carefully planned space to accommodate possessions in such a way that all items are easy to see and are within reach for convenient removal and replacement.

A commitment to environmental concerns is important to today's families. Recycling has become a part of life, and receptacles should be incorporated into every kitchen design. Energy conservation includes evaluating energy efficiency ratings among different appliances, and considering "life cycle" costs when making all purchase decisions. Life cycle costs are computed by totaling the purchase price, installation expense, yearly energy costs, and anticipated maintenance charges. This number is then divided by the years of service the appliance (or countertop, or set of cabinets) is expected

Ellen Cheever, Heritage Custom Kitchens: Warm, natural colors provide a soothing backdrop for food preparation and socializing. Recessed ring pulls enhance the clean lines of the cabinetry.
▲

DeWitt Talmadge Beall:
A large skylight pours natural
illumination onto work surfaces
and lends a bright, airy feeling
to the entire space.

◀

to provide. Smart shoppers will often find that items considered to be expensive, when evaluated solely by initial purchase price, prove to be the most affordable when rated by "life cycle" costs.

Entertainment and information are being brought into the kitchen as well. The kitchen may even include its own small TV, radio, and specialized sound system, allowing cooks to catch up with the news or enjoy their favorite music while chopping and slicing. Ensuring all equipment is equally accessible to cooks and visitors may entail preparing special wiring plans, specifying customized cabinetry and considering the viewing angle from different parts of the room.

With today's more informal lifestyle, families often prefer an eating area within the kitchen for their daily meals, reserving the dining room for special occasions and holiday meals. Custom tables attached to islands, or tables incorporated into wall areas or peninsulas are replacing "standard" counter dining to produce a cozy setting where diners can face one another without wasting an inch of precious space.

Because accessibility and safety for all potential users is a top planning priority, counters with rounded corners, appliances with easy-to grab handles, safety locks on select storage cabinets, legible appliance controls, and microwave ovens placed at reasonable heights are design considerations when developing a kitchen to accommodate multi-generational families sharing a variety of tasks.

EXPERTISE, EXPERIENCE AND EMPATHY

As you've seen, the re-definition of how we live and how we use our kitchens has led to new and innovative approaches to design. Because this all-important room must be comfortable, accommodating, efficient, safe and inviting, choosing the right designer probably has never been more important.

The role of the kitchen designer has changed as significantly as the kitchen itself. The increased complexity associated with kitchens demands more technical expertise as well as the vision of a specialist whose daily focus is on how the kitchen is used.

What has not changed is the important role a design professional can play in protecting your

Rutt of New York City: Prairie pine is an ideal complement to rustic or country settings. The informal feel is achieved further by incorporating exposed plate storage racks.

▲

interests. For many homeowners, building or remodeling a kitchen is a once in a lifetime experience. Professional expertise, especially at the planning stages – even if you know what you want – is essential. It is a relationship that will save you money, headaches and heartache.

What should you look for in a kitchen specialist? Since this person will be designing a total multi-purpose living environment for you, your best choice is an experienced professional who offers a multi-dimensional, comprehensive approach to kitchen design. The best in the business are artists who understand all styles and can work with them comfortably. Avoiding style dictates from fashion gurus, they are consummate professionals not limited by their own individual preferences. They are interpreters who closely listen to you and evaluate what you want and what you need.

nuHaus: Bold architectural pillars beautifully frame the entrance to a dramatic kitchen that deserves to be the most livable room in the house.

▶

These designers must be navigators, space planners and comparative shoppers who maneuver you through the technical maze of product selections. By prioritizing your preferences, they work within your budget and consistently prove that budget constraints do not doom a project to mediocrity. They are value-oriented specialists who match product quality levels to your needs. Rather than indulging in wasteful "over-engineering", they tailor the design solution, product mix and installation schedule to fix your individual project.

The finest kitchen specialists are methodical technicians who can supervise the preparation of clear, understandable plans and project documents, and ensure the correct interpretation of these documents once the job is underway. They are global citizens who weave responsible resource management throughout the product selection process and continue it with specific usage recommendations. Using principles of universal design, they will create a room appropriate for your family with attention to any specialized requirements you may have.

What's the best way to find these highly-qualified specialists? As with any search for a service professional, the best resources are friends and acquaintances. Speak with people who have remodeled and ask for recommendations. Such an endorsement is invaluable because an actual example of a professional's work is far more telling than simple words of promise from an unproven stranger.

Once you start working with a designer, express yourself! Your designer can only create your dream room if you share your vision. Be prepared to identify clearly what you like. Collect pictures of materials, layouts, designs or styles that grab your attention. Visit different showrooms and study portfolios of actual projects. Scrutinize the style, execution, and creativity with a keen eye for identifying what appeals to you and what does not.

Don't assume well-known design professionals only work on large scale projects. Discuss the budget set aside for the project early in the planning stages. If you haven't any idea about what a realistic investment figure is for the room under consideration, tell the designer. A specialist is an experienced expert

Kitchen Classics, Inc.:
Everything's looking up in
this space-age kitchen with its
unusual arrow-shaped cabinetry
and contrasting white and
black tile.
▲

nuHaus: Details, details. Outside light streams through glass mullioned door cabinets that reflect and reinforce this home's airy architecture. Note also the subtle relationships between design details: the curvature of the countertop to the cased archways, for instance, and the valance pattern in the cabinets to the support bracket under the countertops.

bulthaup (LA) Inc:
Material selection varies
according to the functions
within a kitchen. Here,
wood and stone is used
in the preparation area;
steel is used for cooking.

▲

who can show you similar projects and will discuss openly the required investment.

A good designer can take any room and create a basic functional workspace, a room with custom touches important to your family, or a space which expresses your own signature style. Each approach requires a different investment on your part. One of the best services a kitchen professional can provide is to help prioritize your "want list" into practical and monetary terms. Nearly every project has limitations, particularly on money and available space. The true professional will help you allocate funds based on your priorities for your dream kitchen.

A professionally-designed kitchen can represent a significant investment, but it makes excellent financial sense. It pays off – both as you enjoy your home and when you sell it. In fact, studies consistently indicate sellers are likely to realize a nearly 100% return on investments in kitchen renovations. Almost as important, a home with a good kitchen will sell faster than one without.

I began my career in California, planning kitchens for homeowners in the city of Sacramento and the surrounding countryside. Now, as a veteran with over twenty years as a kitchen designer, it is a pleasure to share with you my thoughts on contemporary kitchen design.

My work as a design professional has led me to plan wonderful kitchen and bath projects for valued clients throughout the world. Recently, in addition to design work for individual families, my efforts focused on the specific elements needed for modern kitchen planning. During my tenure with the National Kitchen and Bath Association, I spearheaded much of the research studying people's behavior and preferences as well as work patterns, clearances for appliances, and different methods of storage – all essential to planning a well-executed kitchen. Ultimately, these studies became the basis for the new planning standards and were published in manuals and books explaining the new guidelines in design.

Throughout my career I have found that, regardless of the size of the project or complexity of the design challenge, clients always provide a wealth of inspiration for their own projects. I am also continually inspired by the exceptional work of my respected colleagues, many of whom are represented in this book.

As you enjoy these beautiful examples of outstanding designs, you'll see just how far the kitchen has come from those yesteryear scenes of daily drudgery. It has truly been transformed into the heart and soul of family living space. My best wishes to you as you create your dream kitchen. I think you'll find the new space will add to your enjoyment of your home, your family, and life itself.

Ellen Cheever, Heritage Custom Kitchens: A combination of furniture finishes on the cabinetry creates an elegant, formal kitchen. Polished granite on the island is combined with easy-to-care-for solid-surface worktops in the sink area. A hand-painted tile mural in the cooking niche adds a splash of color and personal touch to the kitchen.

▲

American Classic Kitchens, Inc.
150 East 58th Street
New York, NY 10155
P 212.838.9308   F 212.838.9318

A vision of the future, this kitchen achieves a high-tech look by combining a deep cherry finish with high-gloss white polyester. Note also the generous use of stainless steel, the sandblasted glass island top, and the absolute black counters.

▲

This hutch is right at home in a Midwestern farmhouse. The distressed pine is highlighted by the white build up typical of Wood-Mode's Heirloom finishes.

▲

American Classic Kitchens is a full-service kitchen design studio that handles projects from design through installation.

Located in the prestigious Architects and Designers Building in New York, the company's 3,000-square-foot showroom displays seven kitchens illustrating the wide range of offerings available from Wood-Mode Cabinetry. Visitors see the latest in appliances, cabinetry and countertops in looks ranging from English Country to sleek European contemporary.

The talented staff of designers and installers is led by Anna Mesaikos, president, who spent her formative years immersed in the arts and surrounded by a family of artists, an upbringing that laid the ground work for her design career.

Mesaikos is drawn to the challenge of space conceptualization. Designing highly functional, flexible and yet artistically fashioned kitchens allows her to give full rein to her interests in art and design.

AMERICAN CLASSIC KITCHENS

◄

The traditional look of the doors is achieved by spraying a white finish over red oak that has been sealed to reveal only a subtle grain. Dark pine shelves provide contrast with the white cabinetry and consistency with the dark tile liners on the walls. The copper hood - the focal point of the kitchen - appears to be suspended in air on a "flyover" shelf over the cooktop.

▲

Inspired by quaint English farmhouses, this natural maple kitchen is at home in practically any setting. Raised door panels complement a unique combination of rope moldings and a dentil cornice to provide delicate balance. The dark granite top accentuates the detailing in the cabinetry, while the herringbone travertine floor provides its own interest.

 ◀ ▲

A classic American kitchen perfect for entertaining. The exaggerated raised panel is found in few cabinet lines.

Here, the two hob units have been stepped forward to become the kitchen's centerpiece. Mullion door cabinets with glass shelves and halogen spotlights provide the ultimate showcase for the family china. Combined with verde marble and polished brass, this kitchen is the ultimate statement of sophistication and international lifestyle.

▲

Beacon Hill, Wood-Mode's most detailed cabinetry line, fits snugly under the low beams in this 16th century cottage. The exuberant spirit of the French countryside finds expression in the beaded paneling, turned posts and hand-carved appliques. Note the stunning jade green Viking range and the antique floor border, which is repeated in hand-painted stencils on the walls.

Anne K. Donahue Interior Design
2818 Pelham Place
Hollywood, CA 90068
P 213.957.1960   F 213.962.5973

Anne K. Donahue

Anne Donahue graduated from the interior design program of the University of Arizona in Tucson and completed special studies at the University of Copenhagen Royal Academy of Architecture and Design. She has specialized in kitchens since 1984 and is a member of the American Society of Interior Designers and the International Furnishings and Design Association.

Donahue's work has been published in several national and local publications such as *Home Magazine, Woman's Day Kitchen and Bath*, and *Southern California Home and Garden*. She also has received the Du Pont Corian Kitchen Design Award. Donahue has also participated in the Pasadena Showcase House of Design, as well as other showcase houses.

Though the bulk of her work is in California, Donahue has designed kitchens throughout the country. Her international experience includes projects in Mexico City, Tokyo and Banff, Canada.

Donahue specializes in working closely with her clients, interpreting their needs and tastes, and creating an environment that best suits their lifestyle. Her emphasis in kitchen design is on creating a functional space for everything.

The breakfast area in this kitchen provides a practical spot to do some transplanting or a sunny spot to enjoy a meal.

Glass door fronts make it easy to see much of the kitchen's contents at a glance. Brightly colored packaged goods and pottery become part of the overall design.

▲

Under-counter drawers have molded inserts to hold cutlery tidily. Narrow drawers with pleasing dovetail edges keep items such as foil and wax paper at hand under the cooktop.

◄

Among Siematic's numerous custom-cabinet features, the ample pantry is a standout. Its spacious interior shelves pivot to reveal additional storage on the back sides. Sturdy chrome guardrails hold even the smallest cans securely in place.

Under-cabinet carousels take full advantage of a corner that might otherwise be dead space.

▼

An angled drawer insert for spices prevents light damage and protects bottles from grease, two big disadvantages of the usual open spice rack.

▶

Bartcrest
150 East 58th Street, 8th Floor
New York, NY 10155
P 212.838.4884   F 212.838.4936

Bartcrest USA Ltd. has been in the kitchen design business since 1988. President Robert Hughes has more than 10 years of experience designing SieMatic kitchens. In 1992, Bartcrest added Smallbone to its line of kitchen furniture.

The company has designed and installed kitchens in many of Manhattan's most exclusive apartment buildings, as well as in Florida, the U.S. Virgin Islands, Mexico, St. Maarten and Saudi Arabia.

Bartcrest's professional staff includes skilled craftsmen and Smallbone and SieMatic designers. The company's designs have been featured in *House & Garden, House Beautiful, Interior Design* and *Metropolitan Home.*

Featuring handpainted Smallbone cabinetry, this kitchen was designed for a Manhattan townhouse by John Herbert.

▲

A fusion of craftsmanship and design, this inlay kitchen uses traditional joinery construction with rail and stile paneled doors set into solid wooden frames. Handmade from sycamore, the cabinet doors feature a boxwood and walnut inlay in a geometric design.

Note the sophisticated combination of pale sycamore, black granite worktops, and stainless steel. The desk has a folding flap and drawer useful for organizing the household's affairs.

▶

B ARTCREST

◀

This SieMatic kitchen was
installed in a townhouse on Park
Avenue in New York City.

▲

Once the room of Sara Roosevelt (FDR's mother — the portrait is said to be of her), this room now serves several purposes — kitchen, casual dining, sitting area and study. There's even a dog kennel built into the handsome Smallbone cabinetry.

▲

Note the mixture of thrift shop finds like the sofa and slipper chair with fine antiques like the Thomas Hope black gilt Regency arm chair, circa 1815. The room was designed by Eric D.W. Cohler Inc.

▲

Barbara Ostrom Associates designed this pantry (using SieMatic products) for the 1993 Kips Bay Designer Showhouse.

◄

Designed by Ann Morris, CKD, the kitchen in this Palm Beach, Florida, home had been three different rooms when the house was built in 1925. Since the homeowners enjoy entertaining and spending time in the kitchen, they wanted a functional space that also would be aesthetically pleasing and comfortable.

DeWitt Talmadge Beall
4277 Murietta Avenue
Sherman Oaks, CA 91423
P 818.907.6039 F 818.905.9891

DeWitt Talmadge Beall

A kitchen is as practical as a knife or a spoon. Its shape should derive from what we ask it to do. Beyond that, it's a question of personal style. The bones of a good kitchen remain the same.

Style, they say, is your mind's voice – the way you express yourself, what you're comfortable being in and living with.

Today there are a bewildering array of styles and choices in cabinetry, appliances, countertops, lighting, flooring, and architectural details.

After 40 years in the business, I've seen a lot of solutions, both practical and aesthetic. No two kitchens are exactly alike, and the process continues to keep me on my toes, which is one of the things I like about it. I enjoy the creative dialogue with architects, interior designers, and clients, and seek to bring to each project freshness, reliability, and good sense.

A kitchen or bath is a long-term investment. It should wear well. My thrust is to find the best solution permitted by the space, the budget, and the needs of your life.

All photography by Paul E. Sharp

DeWitt Talmadge Beall

Benvenuti & Stein, Inc.
Geno Benvenuti
2001 Greenleaf Street
Evanston, IL 60202
P 708.866.6868   F 708.866.8010

Geno Benvenuti

Master bath renovation utilizing unused attic space. Brass accents complement the Carrera white and Verde Alpe marble composition.

▶

Benvenuti & Stein has been providing the finest design/build services available on Chicago's North Shore since 1977. Our success and continued growth stems from the basic philosophy that all 34 members of our staff share: "The desire to do creative, distinctive, high quality work with the utmost attention to detail."

I get a great deal of satisfaction developing the most exciting design solution possible. Often it is one the client had never considered. My staff of architects and designers, carpenters and cabinetmakers provides the framework of experience and knowledge crucial in creating and redefining the details as a project is transformed from a drawing to reality.

To achieve and maintain our standard of craftsmanship, we purposely limit the quantity of projects we undertake each year. I initially meet with every client we do business with, then direct the development of each design and visit the site regularly to watch over the fine details as our carpenters build the space. Our design department and cabinet shop work together, under one roof, where every piece of trim and cabinetry is custom made. This combination of talents assures our clients of the best possible result and the comfort in knowing that their project is under control from start to finish.

Over the years, our projects have repeatedly been chosen for publication in *Better Homes & Gardens, Kitchen & Bath Quarterly, Remodeled Homes* and other national and local publications.

BENVENUTI & STEIN, INC.

◀

Natural wood tones warm the room and provide a pleasant contrast to the white cabinets. This composition reflects what might have been designed when the home was built in 1908, with some very contemporary features. A pantry, powder room, back staircase, mud room, and small porch surrounding the original 11' by 9' kitchen were combined to create this family space.

▲

Kitchen renovation combining
two smaller rooms that allows
for an efficient work space and
a standard height table.

◀

An antique chest refurbished for
an island becomes the focal
point of this classic white
kitchen.

▶

Solid Honduran mahogany vanity, with matching wainscot panels and columns surround the whirlpool, creating an elegant way to start or end one's day.

Rolltop desk and a split pantry cabinet provide a home-office space conveniently located near the table.

The space artfully blends traditional and contemporary elements.

bulthaup (LA) Inc
153 South Robertson Boulevard
Los Angeles, CA 90048
P 310.288.3875   F 310.288.3885

Chris Tosdevin

An international company based in Germany, bulthaup has achieved an enviable reputation for kitchen quality and innovation. Its United States operation is based in Los Angeles, home to an exclusive showroom that reflects the company's strong emphasis on function and the use of different materials.

Chris Tosdevin, president, trained as an interior designer in England, and has worked with bulthaup for over twelve years. His work has been widely published in American and European magazines, including *Elle Decor, Home* and *Interior Design.*

Years of research into professional and domestic cooking led bulthaup to develop its latest product - System 25. This new furniture system addresses current lifestyle needs and confirms that the kitchen has become the focal point of the house. An emphasis on open-plan design heightens the kitchen's role in everyday life by fully integrating it with primary living spaces.

The versatility of bulthaup allows the company to create true working and living environments, each as unique and individual as the clients who commission them. Today, bulthaup is one of the world's leading forces in kitchen design philosophy.

bulthaup

◀

This kitchen reflects the home's role as a focus for entertaining. The atmosphere is informal. Many people can help prepare and cook food, and the primary cook is no longer separated from family and friends. Everyday tasks are pleasurable and easy to perform in a well-designed kitchen.

The materials and dimensions of various finishes complement each other, allowing them to be combined according to their suitability for particular needs. Here, American black cherry - the primary finish - is accented with stainless steel and glass.

▲

This recycling unit allows trash to be sorted easily. Glass, plastic, aluminum and other items are separated into different containers and bins within one pullout. A self-closing lid protects against odors.

◄

Wooden containers of varying sizes can be combined in drawers and pullouts to create custom storage areas. The quality craftsmanship is obvious in the hand-finished corner joints.

This pullout pantry unit with adjustable shelves and railings provides more than 100 pounds of storage capacity and is accessible from all sides. The earthenware container with maple lid allows bread to breathe and keep fresh for days.

The open kitchen and living space has become part of the lifestyle of the '90s. This clean, timeless design combines the practicality of white laminate with the warmth of natural wood. It's arranged with each function in mind, from closed storage for dry goods to glass cabinets for china and stemware. Stainless steel is used below the cooking area due to its ability to repel oil and grease.

Heritage Custom Kitchens
215 Diller Avenue
New Holland, PA 17557
P 717.354.4011 F 717.355.0169

This master bath creates an adult oasis where the sexes can peacefully coexist. Geared to basic grooming, the man's custom vanity features storage areas lined with felt for change, cufflinks and sunglasses. It has a higher counter to make shaving more comfortable. ◀

Ellen Cheever, CKD, CBD, ASID

A design pioneer, Ellen Cheever has helped revolutionize kitchen design over the past 20 years. Under her leadership, research into kitchen and bathroom planning was conducted, leading to new industry design standards.

Widely published for her designs and expertise in kitchen planning, Cheever wrote two highly acclaimed books on kitchen and bath design. While managing her own residential kitchen and bath design firm in California, she worked with clients on the East and West Coasts.

She continues a limited design practice while contributing to the product development and design education for kitchen designers affiliated with Heritage showrooms throughout North America. An internationally recognized kitchen authority, Cheever was recently inducted into the National Kitchen & Bath Association's Hall of Fame.

Cheever considers the kitchen to be the warmest, friendliest room in the home and believes it should be a welcoming space, accommodating all family members. Kitchens, however, are foremost work environments that must be functional. Therefore, efficiency needs to be attained without sacrificing beauty or style.

Listening to the client is crucial to discovering what their kitchen needs to do for them. When her clients look at each other with knowing smiles that their dream has been translated into reality, Cheever knows she has succeeded.

HERITAGE CUSTOM KITCHENS

A combination of furniture finishes on the cabinetry creates an elegant, formal kitchen. Polished granite on the island is combined with easy-to-care-for solid-surface worktops in the sink area. A hand-painted tile mural in the cooking niche adds a splash of color and personal touch to the kitchen.

A message center/desk area, tucked in an alcove, helps organize and conceal paperwork.

▲

Functional storage areas are built into this kitchen. The pantry has pull-out shelves and special doors that fold out of the cook's way. Tall decorative columns pull out, exposing custom areas for kitchen linens and the family's bulletin board.

 ▶

This vanity boasts drawers and storage to accommodate the special needs of a woman. Custom drawer dividers organize makeup and skin-care products on one side and hair and nail paraphernalia on the other. Wall units offer extra deep storage and recessed areas for grooming appliances and jewelry.

Classic white cabinets, combined with an antique baker's table, create a traditional kitchen. Built-in appliances are paneled to match the cabinetry. Solid-surface counter, with an integral sink, provide functional worktops.

Featured at the prestigious Kohler Design Center, this casual French Country style offers cabinetry with fine furniture detailing such as a hand-carved valance, accent moldings, and a special antique glaze finish on the cherry wood.

Cook's Custom Cabinetry
1191 Palmer Wood Court
Sarasota, FL 34236
P 813.366.6112

Ronald G. Cook

Ronald G. Cook, owner and president of Cook's Custom Cabinetry, has more than 34 years of experience planning and designing custom kitchens and other rooms in the home. He has expertise with both American and European cabinetry.

Ron holds degrees in lighting design and kitchen design and is past president of the National Kitchen and Bath Association. He sits on the Advisory Committee for Wood-Mode and the Advisory Council for Sub Zero. He also was selected to serve on the New Products Board of Kitchen-Aid for two years.

Cook's Custom Cabinetry helps clients achieve their personal objectives through technical expertise and quality designs. The company's high standards and thoughtful plans are the cornerstone of its reputation.

COOK'S CUSTOM CABINETRY

Beauty and function create the
utmost in convenience and
workable traffic flow.
Symmetrical, consistent design
produces a feeling of classic
elegance.

The style and design of this "Cook's Kitchen" makes it an inviting gathering place for family and friends.

This kitchen features two distinct work areas and a large "L" shaped serving area, allowing several people to work simultaneously.

This larder room provides an attractive and practical area for storage. Special accents include fluted columns, plinth blocks, rosettes with crown molding.

▶

Fluted columns and granite countertops accent the island food preparation area.

◀

Traditional craftsmanship creates an Old World English country look with carved wood molding that embellishes the cabinetry. Family and friends can gather in the kitchen without disrupting the chef.

▶

Cooper-Pacific Kitchens, Inc.
Pacific Design Center
8687 Melrose Avenue, Suite G-776
Los Angeles, CA 90069
P 310.659.6147   F 310.659.1835

The Cooper-Pacific Kitchens design team

Cooper-Pacific Kitchens is a family business with more than 30 years experience in kitchen design. The company maintains a 7,000-square-foot showroom in the Pacific Design Center and has completed more than 1,500 kitchens throughout the United States. Professional staff includes certified kitchen designers, architectural designers, and technical, administrative and customer service personnel. A warehouse and freight-forwarding facility also is provided as a service to clients.

"International" describes the design themes sought by Cooper-Pacific's multicultural clientele in Southern California.

"We design personal kitchens that meet our clients' needs and reflect their way of living," says Neil Cooper. "Listening and communicating with our clients is the most important part of the design process."

Cooper-Pacific represents the finest products in the world, including SieMatic cabinetry from Germany and Smallbone kitchen furniture from England.

The company has won numerous design awards and has seen its work published in several national and regional publications, including *Better Homes & Gardens, HOME, Metropolitan Home, House Beautiful, Designer's West* and *California Homes & Lifestyles*.

COOPER-PACIFIC KITCHENS

Old World English charm comes to life in this hand-painted kitchen. The open plate rack, pull-out willow baskets and hanging pot rack provide functionality, while enhancing the ambience. A pleasing sense of texture is created by combining black granite countertops with a butcher block island, solid teak drain board around the sink, and hand-painted English backsplash tiles.

An ash island and pot rack add the warmth of wood to this striking contemporary kitchen. Stainless steel open shelves provide storage in place of traditional wall cabinets.

◄

Deep green kirkstone counter- tops accent rich Anegre wood cabinetry in this island setting. The commercial cooktop and hood allow the homeowner the professional cooking capacity she wanted while interacting with family and friends seated at the island.

▼

Column pantries flanking the ovens provide a dramatic design element in this contemporary setting. The radius hood and rounded cabinetry corners echo the home's architecturally soft lines.

►

Black granite counters, bold tile and gold-plated knobs highlight this dramatic kitchen in gloss-white lacquer. The solid maple island top and herringbone oak wood floor add warmth.

▶

This large center island serves as an area for food preparation as well as informal seating for breakfast and snacks.

◀

Dalia Kitchen Design
One Design Center Place, #643
Boston, MA 02210
P 617.482.2566   F 617.482.2744

Dalia Tamari

This older waterfront home features a remodeled kitchen. The challenge: create a small but functional room that blends well with the home's existing space and color scheme.

The transparency of the glass updraft hood allows the cook to maintain eye contact with guests in the adjoining living and dining rooms.

▼

After graduating from the Israel Institute of Technology in 1972, Dalia Tamari worked as an interior designer in Israel, Iran and Singapore. She moved to the United States in 1983 and accepted a position in the New York showroom of Alno of Germany, the world's largest manufacturer of kitchen cabinetry.

In 1986, Tamari opened her own showroom in Boston, which became Alno's top U.S. dealership within three years. In 1992, she became the exclusive northern New England dealer for William Ohs timeless kitchen cabinets.

Having installed more than a thousand kitchens for satisfied customers, Tamari is widely recognized as one of the leading kitchen designers in New England. Her work exhibits a strong European influence, thanks in part to her annual practice of attending design and cabinetry shows in Europe.

Though Tamari has a strong background in cabinetry, she stresses that "we do not sell cabinets, we design kitchens." Tamari's turnkey approach to kitchen design involves helping clients choose cabinetry, appliances, tile, wallpaper, flooring and dining furniture. Her knowledge of trends in each of these design elements is complemented by her command of the latest appliance technology.

DALIA KITCHEN DESIGN

◄

This kitchen was installed in a charming stone house nestled in the forest. Tuscany-style detailing by William Ohs cabinetry creates a unique and romantic, yet practical and sophisticated, kitchen design.

The old-fashioned hood adds a cozy atmosphere around the cooking area. The layout of the kitchen is very efficient, creating a warm gathering place that doubles as an excellent space for the individual gourmet cook.

▲

"Salisbury pink" granite countertops complement the light tone of the cabinets.

◄

This kitchen addition features a tile floor and spruce-colored cabinets with raised panels.

▼

The adjacent family room is two steps lower than the kitchen. A peninsula in the family room backs up to the kitchen cabinets and serves as a bar. The kitchen ▼ was designed to be especially bright and airy, an important benefit since the homeowner spends a lot of time cooking.

A beautiful view awaits bathers
in this luxurious oasis.

▲

The kitchen in this weekend home in New Hampshire is often used by a number of cooks at once, so it was designed to accommodate a heavy traffic flow easily. One side of the kitchen serves as a storage area – cold storage in the Sub-zero refrigerator and dry storage in a large pantry. Another wall is designed as a cleaning center in which the sink, dishwasher and trash compactor are located. The remaining wall is used as a preparation center.

▲ ▼

de Giulio kitchen design, inc.
1121 Central Avenue
Wilmette, IL 60091
P 708.256.8833   F 708.256.8842

674 North Wells Street
Chicago, IL 60610
P 312.337.2700   F 312.337.6196

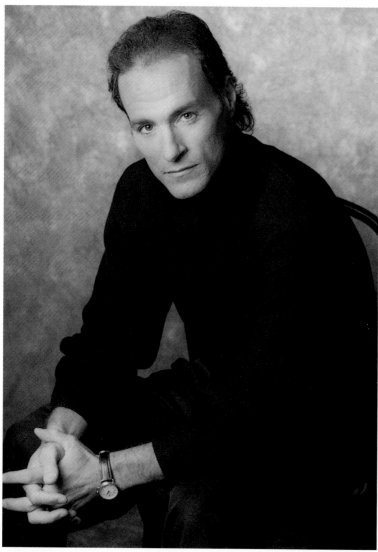

Mick De Giulio

de Giulio kitchen design, inc. has more than 20 years of experience designing and installing kitchens. The firm maintains two showrooms in the Chicago area and has installed nearly 1,000 kitchens across the country.

de Giulio employs 30 professionals, including designers, architects, artisans and service staff. In addition, Mick's work has been published in countless magazines, including *House Beautiful, Traditional Home, Good Housekeeping and Better Homes & Gardens.*

Mick's philosophy of design revolves around "creating an enhanced, total living environment individually suited for each client." His staff's ability to establish easy working rapport with clients allows even the most discriminating client to be attended with tenacious determination for perfection.

The architecture and style of de Giulio's kitchens integrate advanced interior design solutions that are timeless, functional and innovative. By searching the world over, de Giulio finds the best materials to achieve superior results, including SieMatic and Smallbone cabinetry.

Each de Giulio-designed kitchen reflects the client's preferences and lifestyle, resulting in designs that are original, elegant and timeless.

A kitchen is not merely
functional. Hand-painted,
free-standing cupboards and
niches, created with special
thought, give each space its
own personality.

Separate areas dedicated to food preparation, cooking and clean-up allow several people to work together simultaneously. The multi-surface island offers another approach to this concept, permitting the homeowner to perform many tasks in one place. Ample storage - without heavy wall cabinetry - is provided by the plate and pot racks.

Both contemporary and Old World charm come together through the use of stainless steel and tumbled marble tile. Unique storage provides easy access to cooking utensils.

The central island, coupled with a commercial-style range, does double duty as either a food-preparation space or informal dining area, making it easy for family and friends to gather with the homeowners.

▶

The blending of modern style and craft traditions highlights this naturally lit kitchen. The balance is achieved through the use of a coffered wood ceiling. Its pattern is reflected in the marble floor and is complemented by glass-fronted cabinets.

▲

Contrasting materials of dark wood and stainless steel create an inviting family environment amid a contemporary setting. This kitchen provides enough storage, preparation area and seating for a group of any size.

▼

Designs Unlimited, Inc.
5 Parker Road
Osterville, MA 02655
P 508.428.3999   F 508.420.3640

A vanity with all the features: pullout towel bar, ample drawer storage, and pullout hamper.

◄

Thomas F. Leckstrom, CKD, President

For more than 25 years, Kitchen & Bath Designs Unlimited, Inc. has designed cabinetry for beautiful homes throughout New England. Located in the quaint Cape Cod village of Osterville, the company works with the area's outstanding architects and custom home builders, as well as directly with homeowners. Many of its clients are the sons and daughters of previously satisfied customers.

President, Thomas F. Leckstrom is a Certified Kitchen Designer, accredited through the National Kitchen and Bath Association. His work has been published in prestigious magazines such as *Architectural Digest, Design Times* and *Cape Cod Life*.

At Designs Unlimited, the preferences, lifestyle and functional requirements of clients are the driving influences behind the company's designs. This client involvement is central to Leckstrom's philosophy, along with the need to create a feeling of harmony between space and materials within the design itself.

Leckstrom believes each kitchen and bath is an investment that will reap benefits now and in the future. In keeping with the Yankee tradition of thrift, he establishes realistic budgets with clients - and stays within those parameters.

A world of design ideas and architectural styling featuring Heritage Custom Kitchens cabinetry can be found in the Designs Unlimited showroom.

DESIGNS UNLIMITED, INC.

Traditional white-painted cabinetry is softened by the use of antiques and baskets. Bright blue tiles in the backsplash bring the colors of the ocean indoors. The center island is designed to hold the grill, store cookbooks, and provide seating for informal gatherings.

▲

64

Old World antique pine cabinetry complements solid-surface counters. The color and texture of the tumbled marble tiles on the backsplash blend with the center island of solid granite, helping to create a very special Cape Cod country kitchen.

◀

This unique kitchen is in the base of a turret. The walls are circular, so the kitchen needed to be designed around a central point. Oyster-white paint on the cabinetry and blue-pearl granite countertops work well with the beautiful ocean vistas.

▶

This hutch area is an attractive focal point across from the work area. Tall pantries are a highly efficient way to store food.

This bath oasis has a steam shower in marble. The whirlpool tub is centered on a spacious window overlooking Nantucket Sound, allowing bathers to float their cares away.

A frost stain softens the strong grain of pecan wood. The custom-designed wood hood is flanked by glass-door cabinets, and the solid-surface counter-tops complement the tiles.

The Frey Company
820 Monroe Avenue NW, Suite 5
Grand Rapids, MI 49503
P 616.456.1220 F 616.456.7677

Rodney Lee TeSlaa

Richard Whallon

C. J. VanDaff

Ronald E. Frey, ASID

The design process is an educational journey that integrates the needs of clients with the appropriate elements of design. As a full-service interior design firm, The Frey Company uses innovative solutions to the complex challenges of kitchen and bath design.

Ron and his staff strive as a team to ensure the identity of their clients be projected in the interiors designed for them. The firm's rapid growth is largely a result of its commitment to reflecting the interests and tastes of each client.

The ability to design in a broad range of styles, accompanied by a working relationship built on integrity and trust, contributes to the successful completion of exciting and enduring interiors.

◀

This kitchen nestled within a contemporary cottage demanded convenience in a stylish setting. The cottage appeal lingers, and so will you as you enjoy working and living amid maple cabinets, checkerboard tile, scrubbed pine doors, and maintenance-free countertops.

Summer colors complemented by natural light evoke the feeling of relaxing weekends at the cottage.

A fluid-patterned wallcovering soothes the angular architecture of this inviting master bath.

The integration of kitchen, family room and dining room makes this space a hub of activity. The openness encourages informal conversation to flow from room to room.

This kitchen renovation transformed a drab, colorless space into a sophisticated, cozy gathering place where elegant antiques and casual country pieces are both welcome.

Hand-painted walls, original watercolors, ceramic tile, and tapestry fabric give this newly constructed bath an Old World charm.

This adaptation of a country French kitchen reaches for the future without letting go of the past. A dark-satin cherry floor, farm-style table, beadboard, and galley railing blend with modern conveniences such as a recycling center, solid-surface counters, a multi-function island, and broad expanses of glass.

Hagerman Design Group
2331 Jolly Road
Okemos, MI 48864
P 517.347.8824
  517.882.2599

Dave Hagerman, CKD

Hagerman Design Group opened its studio in 1993 to showcase kitchen interior design at its best. Principal Dave E. Hagerman, CKD, has designed kitchens for more than 20 years. His work has appeared in several national magazines, including *Home, Country Home, Money, Woman's Day Kitchen and Bath, The Frugal Gourmet's Whole Family Cookbook and West Sampler.*

Hagerman's designs have been recognized with many national awards. He is a two-time recipient of the National Kitchen and Bath Association's James Foster Silver Bowl, the most prestigious kitchen design award in North America. In 1992, Hagerman was named a "Top Fifty Achiever" by *Remodeling* magazine.

Hagerman became a "certified" kitchen designer in 1984. He is president of the National Kitchen and Bath Association's Michigan chapter and a member of the organization's National Board of Governors for Societies. Hagerman also writes design articles for *Kitchen and Bath Business.*

He has been honored to work with clients such as Jeff Smith, "The Frugal Gourmet." Hagerman designed "The Whole Family Kitchen" mentioned in Smith's cookbook. His knowledge of architecture and interior design gives Hagerman Design Group the necessary direction to work with clients throughout the United States who need distinctive kitchens.

HAGERMAN DESIGN GROUP

◀

This kitchen was fashioned for a
gourmet chef. Soapstone sinks,
cherry wood, tin ceiling and two
work stations mix the old and
the new.

▲

This showpiece sink features a pitcher pump that really works. Mounted on the soapstone surface, it takes you to days gone by. Simply turn a tap, and cold water comes from the pump or hot water from a hot water dispenser.

A butler's pantry with cherry and glass doors showcase the homeowner's pewter and glassware collections. The stainless-steel top trimmed with cherry complement the tin ceiling.

▲

Light gray and metal give a contemporary look to this glitzy galley kitchen.

A brick tower housing stainless-steel cooking ovens allow openness yet divides the dining area from the cooking area. To the left is an antique Irish press. Its architectural detail complement the rich Heritage cabinets.

A formal kitchen offers an arts-and-crafts feel through the use of granite counters, wainscot and tile backsplash. The cooking center gives the warm feeling of a hearth.

This cooking station allows space to visit with family and friends while preparing food. The center is raised to hide the range's venting system.

James R. Irving, ASID
13901 Shaker Boulevard
Cleveland, OH 44120
P 216.283.1991
216.751.1100

James R. Irving, ASID

James R. Irving, ASID has more than 30 years of design experience in the United States and abroad.

Irving is renowned as a colorist decorator of the unique and unusual. His attention to detail makes his work extraordinary. He has designed many showcase homes and has been published in numerous books, newspapers and magazines, including *Colonial Homes, Victorian Homes* and *Cleveland Magazine.*

Irving attended Western Reserve University, The New York School of Interior Design, and the Institute of Rome, Italy. He believes the kitchen and bath are the heart of the home and should be as personal as possible.

The juxtaposition of antiques, color and space create visual treats in Irving's work and help his clients achieve the ultimate lifestyle.

A lovely window reflects the heart of the kitchen and garden in this sophisticated town house.
▼

A unique pantry and storage area enhance the function of a country French kitchen.
▲

JAMES R. IRVING, ASID

◀

This sophisticated bathroom
brings a dash of Palm Beach
drama to a Shaker Heights,
Ohio, home.

▲

A stylish kitchen adds an extra degree of enjoyment to cooking and entertaining in Shaker Heights.
◀

A wonderful view is always on the menu in this breakfast room in Bratenahl.
▼

Rare and exotic antique porcelains peer over the granite counter of a high-rise kitchen.
▲

A country sitting room/kitchen features all the accouterments of function and style.
◀

Double sinks, a skylight and vibrant color create a dazzling effect.
▲

Antiqued woods and tablesetting create a European atmosphere.
▶

Jane Page Creative Designs, Inc.
200 Westcott
Houston, TX 77007
P 713.803.4999   F 713.803.4998

The ceiling was raised and stepped, the window was enlarged, and a custom "torn" paper was applied to the ceiling and walls, adding color and texture to this dramatic remodeling project.

◀

Jane Page Crump, ASID

The creativity and uncompromising standards practiced by Jane Page Creative Designs, Inc. have made this firm one of the most respected in the industry, widely known for its elegant and distinctive kitchens and interiors.

Jane Page Crump, president and primary designer, has more than 20 years of experience designing and installing interiors. Her primary areas of interest are kitchens, audio/video centers and cabinetry design. Crump's forte is the blending of colors and furnishings with the lifestyles of her clients to create designs that feature timeless, restrained elegance.

Crump is past president of the Houston Gulf Coast Chapter of the American Society of Interior Designers. Her work has been published in many books and periodicals, including *Showcase of Interior Design, Southern Edition; Who's Who in Kitchen Design West; Designer Specifier; Builder/Architect;* and *Kitchen and Bath Business.*

Crump's designs reflect the time she spends discovering the dreams of her clients, researching new products, and attending to the numerous details involved with each project.

"I am very fortunate to have great clients who share a love of life and an appreciation for good design," she says.

JANE PAGE CREATIVE DESIGNS, INC.

The artistic balancing of glazed wheat colors, the mix of inset and traditional tiles, and the repetitive use of curves integrate this kitchen with the home's overall design. With its shaped two-level counter and inset tumbled marble tiles, the island makes a sculptured statement.

Soft colors and a warm wood
floor offer a subdued
background suitable for an
infinite choice of accessories.

Leaded glass doors in this
butler's pantry echo the design
of the stair railing in the entry.

▼

With a flexible lighting design,
this kitchen is ready for work,
play or a romantic meal.
Incandescent lighting, wall
sconces, lighted cabinets and

general down lights are all used,
making it possible to trade
daytime charm for evening
sophistication.

▲

This casual, yet sophisticated,
seating arrangement is perfect
for savoring either coffee or
champagne. The television in
the corner cabinet can be

viewed from anywhere in the
kitchen. Note the elegant touch
provided by the beveled mirror
backsplash.

▼

Rich detail is evident in this traditional kitchen. The elegant mix of finish materials and architectural detailing is tied together by the blue-and-white color scheme.

This contemporary design is achieved by incorporating smooth, reflective surfaces, laminated cabinets and solid-surface countertops. The monochromatic color scheme visually enlarges the space. Vertical shutters separate the entry from the eating area. Meanwhile, glass blocks permit a view of the living room and pool.

Size and shape were the challenges in this 11-foot-square kitchen in a home that was built in 1905 and last remodeled in 1915. Client requirements called for a room that provided ample storage and an elegant dining area. The base and wall-mounted cabinets to the left of the corner television are only 12 inches deep - sufficient for most serving and cooking utensils. The island's pedestal conceals venting and electrical wiring, and the inset rangetop maintains the smooth surface necessary for multiple uses.

Mirrors on the backsplash and pedestal, custom lighting, and large-scale documentary wallcovering play starring roles in bringing this remodeled kitchen beyond modern standards.

Karlson Kitchens
1815 Central Street
Evanston, IL 60201
P 708.491.1300   F 708.491.0100

David Karlson

Innovative cabinetry. Beautiful designs. Exquisite craftsmanship. Excellent customer service. This is what Karlson Kitchens stands for.

A full-service design showroom serving the Chicagoland area for 30 years, Karlson creates kitchens of style and quality. Creativity is key to owner David Karlson. When the company's craftsmen combine years of experience with innovative ideas, the result is a one-of-a-kind design.

At Karlson, customers choose from some of the finest cabinetry the world offers. The company is the exclusive representative in the Midwest for Becker Zeyko, Europe's premier line of cabinetry. Hand-crafted in Germany's Black Forest, Becker Zeyko leads the industry in environmentally friendly products.

Karlson is especially proud of the Becker Zeyko "Idea Workshop" – a full-scale design program that allows clients to literally see their kitchen come to life. Karlson also designs innovative spaces and cabinetry for all other rooms in the home.

"The entire staff at Karlson works with our clients to incorporate all their needs, wants and ideas," says David Karlson. "We create the room of your dreams – a place where memories are made."

Proper design should make a kitchen both functional and beautiful. Here, wood, glass and steel combine to create an elegant ambience that leaves room for personal style. On the left, the "waving" line softens the cabinet architecture. On the right, a decorative ensemble adds a unique focal point.

▲

KARLSON KITCHENS

◀

"Avance" is harmonious
perfection in every possible
way. The cabinets have no
handles, and the result is the
cleanest, sleekest, most ultra-
modern look. Subtle finger
channels provide easy access
to abundant storage space.

▲

Becker Zeyko's "Modula" line stands out through its design and use of color. Door panels are available in blue-green, cobalt blue, ruby red, black or sandblasted wire glass, providing a way to add individuality, brilliance and style to any room.

◀

"Padua" cabinets offer a unique look. The natural, brushed and antique-blue stained surfaces testify to this kitchen's singularity.

▶

Natural-colored maple laminate produces a subtle glow and lively feel in "Plano." The handles are delicately blended into the symmetrical and horizontal lines of these high-styled cabinets. Sleekness and streamlined simplicity are the hallmarks of this kitchen.

◄

Becker Zeyko kitchens even shine behind their handsome doors. The company's waste containers feature hygienic, easy-to-clean separation devices. A locked cage secures toxic substances.

▲ ◄

"Maison" is nature at its best. Smooth fronts in solid alderwood contrast with the rounded handles. An innovative range hood and a beautiful, yet functional, island further enhance this elegantly simple design. Handsome sliding doors with translucent glass are another interesting and unique addition.

►

Kitchen & Bath Concepts
11444 Alpharetta Highway
Roswell, GA 30076
P 404.442.9845   F 404.664.3674

This Craft-Maid English country kitchen displays a distressed bleached and limed finish on white oak, creating an antique-like atmosphere. Fluted columns, plate racks and open display areas contribute to an inviting and functional preparation area.

▲

Kitchen & Bath Concepts is the source for award-winning designs, unique products and professional installation throughout the South. Its 5,000-square-foot showroom in the Atlanta suburb of Roswell is one of the finest in the Southeast.

Thirty years of combined experience in design, manufacturing, construction and installation lie behind the success of Kitchen & Bath Concepts. The team includes trained professionals with design degrees and experienced installation crews.

The company has received regional and national design awards and has been published in numerous magazines. Membership in professional organizations such as the National Kitchen and Bath Association enhances the staff's product knowledge and professionalism.

Kitchen & Bath Concepts creates professional design solutions by first interpreting the lifestyle needs of its clients. Working as a team, designers listen to clients and guide them through the selection process, integrating style and function with colors, finishes, design details, woods and accessories.

The company's use of quality materials, suppliers and contractors is indicative of its attention to detail from design through supervision of the project's installation.

The creations of Kitchen & Bath Concepts are timeless reflections of style, unifying materials, construction and form.

KITCHEN & BATH CONCEPTS

◄

Various textures and architectural elements illustrate how
every detail counts in this
elegant bath. Note the striking
combination of granite,
Craft-Maid cabinets and
gold highlights.

Chrome accents interplay with the continuous curves of the sleek, high-gloss European cabinets by Corsi. With understated simplicity, the rounded DuPont Corian countertop guides traffic through the work triangle.

◀

Contemporary form follows function in this uncluttered design.

▶

Double ovens provide several cooking options and fit smoothly into a brick wall niche highlighted with a faux finish.

▲

The central island integrates storage space, food preparation, cooking, and informal dining. The shape and two levels of the island provide interest and define traffic patterns.

▲

Complete renovation in this master suite created a sophisticated retreat. Luxurious Rojo Alicante marble surrounds the whirlpool tub, vanity tops and steam shower. Finishing details include gray-painted oak vanity cabinets, a brass towel warmer and leaded glass windows.

▶

Mirrors above this vanity help expand the sense of light and space.

▶

Detailed with dentil moulding, open pilasters, spice drawers and an Old World finish, this hutch by Craft-Maid is a distinctive focal point.

▲

Kitchen Classics, Inc.
519 Fourth Street
Wilmette, IL 60091
P 708.251.9540   F 708.251.8770

Ed Hillner

Since 1975, Kitchen Classics, Inc. has designed and executed quality kitchen installations as unique and special as its clients. Each project reflects the tastes and lifestyles of the homeowners. Principals Ed and Nancy Hillner and their staff of seven dedicated professionals have chosen to remain small to give customers the personal care and attention they deserve.

The Hillners believe the kitchen is the heart of every home. They develop kitchens for people who do not simply wish to spend their money, but rather to invest it sensibly. At Kitchen Classics, style and function are standards of equal value, not opposites.

Each project is approached with fresh enthusiasm backed by years of experience. From initial planning sessions to final finishing touches, Kitchen Classics provides quality without compromise. The company blends the practical with the attractive, offering distinctive woods, laminates and lacquers for every taste from Old World to high-tech, along with interior fittings that represent the latest in kitchen technology.

From a tiny architectural millhouse in the Midwest to a world-renowned European manufacturer, diverse suppliers help Kitchen Classics offer each customer styling perfection and functional innovation.

Located in an interior space with no natural light source, this kitchen relies on liberal artificial lighting from overhead recessed cans and undercabinet task lights to provide a bright work area. Enhancing the crisp, sleek appearance are multiple reflective surfaces.

This classic English kitchen combines homey comfort and modern efficiency. Its warm, friendly shades of antiqued pine provide a cozy retreat for family, while its nooks and crannies showcase the homeowner's collectibles.

Since wood is a product of nature, each piece has its own unique characteristics of color and grain. Here, natural wood charm is enhanced by a 15-step finishing process that results in a warm, inviting patina. The walnut pegs and richly molded door frames add subtleties of texture and color to this timeless cottage look.

These cabinet doors are fashioned of brushed stainless tambour material. The strong vertical lines and chiseled profile are the perfect companion to the commercial-style refrigerator, ovens and custom stainless-and-black modular hood.

The ultimate in contemporary drama and appeal, this kitchen combines an angular layout with unique materials. It's an exciting example of the marriage between client individuality and designer vision.

Kitchen Concepts, Inc.
-Your Design Experts -
159 Washington Street
Norwell, MA 02061
P 617.878.6542   F 617.878.8109

Cameron M. Snyder, CKD

The design philosophy of Kitchen Concepts, Inc. revolves around the quest of creating environments that truly reflect the personality and lifestyle of our clients. Rather than portray a "signature" style, we sign our work with the values of integrity, quality and professionalism.

Our firm is driven by a sincere commitment to exceed the customer's highest expectations. The most competent and dedicated staff and our partnership with talented allied professionals, ensure final success and total satisfaction.

Owner Cameron M. Snyder, CKD, president of the National Kitchen & Bath Association and a national design instructor, is one of the most recognized leaders in the kitchen and bath industry. His award winning designs have been featured in several trade and consumer magazines.

The legendary AGA cooker in this classic English country kitchen is surrounded by pine cabinetry and a blue-pearl granite top. Note the rich detailing provided by natural cherry accents, custom leaded glass doors, and the hand-painted tile backsplash and mural.

KITCHEN CONCEPTS, INC.

Founded in 1977 as a kitchen specialist, Kitchen Concepts, Inc. soon expanded to the custom design and installation of bathrooms, master suites, entertainment centers and home-offices, by operating as a full-service space planning firm, specializing in residential environments. Design expertise, quality materials, fine craftsmanship, and excellent service are the trademarks of Kitchen Concepts. Here, attention to detail is reflected in the custom carved maple valances, inlaid two-tone Corian top, hand-painted tile backsplash and selection of antique brass hardware.

The trend toward cocooning has led homeowners to invest more into their homes. Today's kitchen, usually open to other rooms, thereby becoming the nucleus of a total living environment.

The kitchen of the 90's, designed for two or more cooks, often includes a wet bar and a functional island that serve as the focal point for social gatherings.

The softness of the off-white cabinetry and the warmth of the wood floors and ceiling enhance the natural beauty of this oceanfront residence. The kitchen, open to the family room, includes a desk area, a double hutch unit and a bar area. The spacious granite topped island serves both as a cleaning and recycling center, as well as an eating area for family and friends.

This traditional New England kitchen was designed around the client's wish for a corner window. The elegant tradition of custom maple cabinetry is married to the convenience of modern built-in appliances and sandstone Corian countertops. The final touch of cinnabar color in the backsplash was carefully chosen to complement the documentary fabric used in the window treatment and the cinnabar tile backsplash.

◀

The functional elegance in this completely renovated environment allows cooking and entertaining without compromising the client's wish for quality and sophistication. An enlarged window over the sink expands the visual length of the room, while the new vaulted ceilings expose the beams, now custom wrapped in mahogany cherry to match the cabinetry. Unaccustomed to compromise, the owners simply chose the best: custom cabinetry with bidet inset and true glass mullion doors, Dakota mahogany granite backsplash and island top, white Corian countertops and sinks, and European appliances.

▶

Kitchen Distributors, Inc.
1309 West Littleton Blvd.
Littleton, CO 80120
P 303.795.0665   F 303.795.0220
1.800.688.0665

Seated (left to right)

Bev Adams, CKD; Esther Hartman, CKD (President)

Standing (left to right)

Jerry Forwood, CKD; Mikel Altenhofen, CKD;

Tom Hartman, CKD; Mont Hartman, ASCD;

Michael Thornton, ASID; Geoffrey King

Kitchen Distributors, Inc. was established in 1953 by P.G. and Esther Hartman and is still owned by the same family today. The company has worked with prestigious clients around the world and has received numerous awards, including national recognition for its designs for the handicapped and disabled. Many of its projects have been showcased in national publications such as *Country Living, Better Homes and Gardens* and *House Beautiful.*

The Hartman's philosophy of old-fashioned service has been passed on to the company's highly trained staff of certified designers, architects and craftsmen. An eye for detail and unique treatments, coupled with meticulous craftsmanship and careful attention to the ideas of clients, results in projects that are indeed works of art.

Kitchen Distributors' Denver showroom is widely acclaimed. More than one visitor has compared it to a fine art museum. The showroom displays an array of high-end cabinetry and appliances, including selections from Heritage, La Cornue, Sub Zero and Gaggenau. Displays are created as entire room environments, complete with details such as lighting, flooring and appointments.

As the social hub of the home, the kitchen presents a design problem of prime importance. It must have the individual stamp of its owner, while seemlessly combining form and function. The design must be timeless. Many kitchens installed more than 30 years ago by Kitchen Distributors are still in beautiful form and continue to function effortlessly.

KITCHEN DISTRIBUTORS, INC.

◀

High-gloss aubergine polyester is combined with natural maple, stainless steel and granite for a striking combination of shapes and finishes. The glass bar top is uniquely set into the granite, defining the eating space and shaping the island. Halogen lighting accentuates the colors and surfaces.

▲

This antique French Vassiliar sideboard is complemented by hand carvings and cabriole feet at the base of the range.

▲

Lower countertops accommodate a shorter cook, while increasing the height and storage capacity of the appliance garage on the preparation center.

◄

The angular peninsula forms the central work area and allows friends to visit, snack or share a drink without disturbing the cook. Glass-front cabinets provide ample storage for the owner's collectibles. Carved valances, sculpted doors and the softened ivory wood finish produce a comfortable, yet elegant, atmosphere.

►

Rope moldings, beaded edges, and an antique glaze on the pine cabinetry make for a quaint English country dining area. The center cabinet doors above the trestle table contain entertainment equipment. They open simultaneously, allowing for full access inside.

The architectural form of step-soffiting is repeated by cascading planes in the cabinets and alternating depths and heights in the countertops. Note the use of geometric shapes and varying surfaces.

Kitchens By Deane, Inc.
1267 East Main Street
Stamford, CT 06902
P 203.327.7008 F 203.975.1949

The design philosophy of Kitchens By Deane, Inc. can be summarized in one sentence: "When it's a Kitchen By Deane, it's your kitchen."

Our designers work with clients to interpret their ideas into perfect rooms. We go the extra mile to make sure everything is completed to satisfaction. As a result, we have earned a high rate of referrals and a strong reputation in Fairfield and Westchester counties in Connecticut and New York.

In 1994, our staff of seven designers won seven awards in the national design competition sponsored by the National Kitchen and Bath Association.

In addition, we earned Heritage's top sales award in 1993. We also carry DBS reproduction cabinetry and Downsview from Canada. Especially popular in older farmhouses and with antique collectors, reproduction cabinetry is made in the time-honored craftsman style.

Kitchens By Deane's showroom in Stamford, Connecticut, features seven kitchens, a library, and a selection of bath cabinetry.

Kitchens By Deane designers have extensive experience in custom design. They share their expertise with one another and are backed by a first-rate support staff and installation team.

Architect and designer collaborated to open up this kitchen to the adjacent family area. Support columns in the center island allow for maximum open space. A strong statement of individuality is reflected through the warm red cabinets, wood floor, sandstone-color countertops, and classic white ceiling trim, backsplash and columns.

▶

KITCHENS BY DEANE, INC.

◀

The two-level step-down counter in the foreground helps avoid a cluttered look. A change in the ceiling height provides a transition into the breakfast area. Note also how the spatial plane is defined by the suspended ceiling lights.

▲

Part of a 1920's carriage house, the narrow rooms in this kitchen presented distinct design challenges. Specially designed cabinets maintain the look of an old-fashioned country kitchen while concealing modern appliances.

Carved wood detailing, especially on the fireplace and above the mantel, bring to mind centuries-old craftsmanship and Old World charm in this cozy library. Note the custom circle design motif on the cabinet doors.

▶

The challenge here was to design an arts and crafts-style kitchen in a turn-of-the-century Victorian house for a tall-family with two active cooks. Ten-foot ceilings, 37-inch countertops, and unusually high cabinets set the scale. The large "L" island with a sink, dishwasher and built-in storage has a natural green-stone granite top that complements the cherry-tone cabinets and maple-planked floor.

The focal point of this kitchen is the earth-green, Adirondack-style backsplash with relief designs of acorns, bark and a bear. Above, the cabinets feature amber-tinted glass doors with an open shelf on top to display a collection of decorative English serving pieces.

▲

Custom tile in rich Mediterranean colors sets off the English country look of handmade pine cabinetry. A row of plants above the cabinets accentuates the high ceiling.

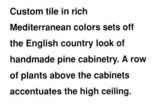

Family gatherings occur spontaneously when the kitchen is the focal point of a home. Here, glass-door cabinets show off dinnerware, a desk area offers cubbyholes for storing small items, and a clever corner bookshelf holds reference books.

▶

Kitchens by Stephanie, Ltd.
2880 Thornhills Avenue, SE
Grand Rapids, MI 49546-7141
P 616.942.9922   F 616.942.9885

Condo kitchens, open by nature yet compact by necessity, often set the tone for the entire unit. The rich navy tile on the counters is used again on the hearth and the transitional white cabinetry flows into a library storage wall.

◄

Stephanie J. Witt, CKD, CBD

My earliest and fondest memories of family and friends center around my childhood kitchen. I remember the most insignificant details...the dancing rainbows cast by the colored glass in a sunny window...parsley and basil growing on the sill, adding the scent of springtime to the cold days of winter. The kitchen was the heart of our home.

It is not surprising that my life's work is creating kitchens. I have a passion for them. My husband and I began focusing our 30 plus years of building experience on kitchens and baths more than a decade ago. At Kitchens by Stephanie, Ltd., we work throughout the home wherever case goods can enhance the decor as well as provide functional storage.

Kitchens by Stephanie, Ltd. is a full service design studio. We hold a state builder's license and are licensed Corian fabricators. I currently serve on the Board of Directors of the National Kitchen and Bath Association. I am a Certified Kitchen Designer as well as a Certified Bath Designer.

At Kitchens by Stephanie, Ltd., our goal is to provide fine quality products, design excellence and superior craftsmanship. It's what you expect, and we never settle for less.

In the words of John Ruskin, "when love and skill work together, expect a masterpiece."

KITCHENS BY STEPHANIE, LTD.

◀

Once a dark, angular, Mediterranean room, this kitchen was transformed using gracious fluid lines with colorful accents enhancing the white cabinets. The circular motif is evident throughout the room as well as on the adjacent raised dining deck. A built-in stereo system fills the area with vibrant sounds, making working and entertaining here a pure delight.

▲

What a delight to design for a sincere gourmet cook! Baking, grilling and broiling all happen frequently in this spacious room of simple elegance. The coffered ceiling successfully encompasses a steel I-beam required for structural support. Peach Corian counters in the food prep and clean-up areas surround the elegant granite center island.

▲

A stately older home with a thoroughly modern kitchen still retains the grace and charm of its original elegance. The high ceilings allow the use of eight foot cabinetry. The rich cherry crown complements the original architectural features of this home.

A Southwest theme highlighting the owner's collection of pottery inspired this floor to ceiling wall of functional storage and display. Rich emerald green walls encompass the mellow tones of the natural maple cabinets.

◄

Kitchensmith, Inc.
3098 Roswell Road
Atlanta, GA 30305
P 404.261.3098

Front Row, Left to Right: Shirley McFarlane, Herb Schmidt, Amie Spencer
Back Row, Left to Right: Don Plott, Lee Woodall, Rodney Urso

Kitchensmith, Inc. has been designing and installing custom kitchens in premier homes throughout the Southeast for 15 years. The firm's beautifully outfitted showroom is located in the prestigious Buckhead area of Atlanta.

Kitchensmith has earned its status as the preferred firm for discriminating clients. Personal attention to details make working with Kitchensmith an exciting, enjoyable experience. Its professional staff of certified kitchen and bath designers has won many local and national design awards, while delivering service that ensures complete client satisfaction.

The newest in design innovations are always available at Kitchensmith so that homeowners can be sure of finding the latest in products and ideas.

Country French styling with dramatic molding and overlays is shown in this very personalized vanity. The Heritage Normandy door style in Hearthstone finish combines an ivory opaque stain with a light brown glaze. The pink marble top with custom edge treatment, decorative bowl and faucet completes this formal bath piece.

▶

KITCHENSMITH

Classic arts and crafts styling is now very current in kitchen design. Here, a light matte bamboo cherry finish enhances Heritage cabinetry. Heart pine flooring and the handmade salt-glazed tile backsplash provide contrast to the built-in Sub-Zero refrigerator and Corian countertops. The stainless finish on the appliances adds a professional touch.

▲

Extensive molding and trim detail are featured in this Gallery Collection cabinetry series by Heritage. The unique combination of a glazed, distressed green stain and a burnished stained maple creates a sophisticated look. Tumbled marble contrasts with the wood backsplash and granite beveled countertop. Antique glass doors allow for accessories or china display. Recessed halogen lighting in the wall cabinetry completes this beautiful Kitchensmith creation.

◀

A rich mahogany finish enhances the warmth of this entertainment area. The Heritage cabinetry features retractable doors for the TV and stereo system. Kitchensmith installed matching paneled walls and moldings to complement the furniture, while allowing considerable concealed storage. Such customization of door styles and finishes has given Kitchensmith an edge in producing the personal living spaces so many homeowners desire.

▶

A kitchen in your living room? This unique kitchen was created for a single individual who desired an entertainment center, living area, dining area and kitchen all in one room - a feat that required the removal of several walls.

When not being used for cooking or serving food, the kitchen closes up and becomes a usable piece of furniture in the living room. Ovens, dishwasher, TV, microwave and toaster oven can all be closed off behind retractable doors. The built-in Sub-Zero refrigerator helps maintain the integrated look of the wall.

An elevated island features deeply recessed bases with a porcelain floor tile in the work area. The absolute black granite counter takes on a coffee table appearance even though it includes a cooktop, sink and faucet.

This Old World Kaufmann door was crafted by Heritage in pine with a white overwash and distressing. The unusual use of small storage niches accents the wall cabinetry above the country porcelain sink. Beaded board backsplash and tile contrast with the solid surface counter and diverter faucet unit. Note the small old iron pulls specified to create an interesting diversion from the wood knobs.

Kitchens Unique By Lois, Inc.
259 Main Street, Box 689
Chester, NJ 07930
P 908.879.6473 F 908.879.2446

Lois M. Kirk

Lois M. Kirk of Kitchens Unique By Lois, Inc. has been designing kitchens and bathrooms for more than 30 years. Her showroom, a stately Victorian house in Chester, New Jersey, is a "second home" to Kirk and three other family members who work together to create fine country and traditional kitchens.

Kirk offers custom-designed kitchens that take into account the taste, special needs, lifestyle and antiques of her clients.

Some of her original designs can be seen in the product manual and sales literature published by Heritage Custom Cabinetry. She has served on the Heritage Design Board and has received national awards, including one from the National Kitchen and Bath Association. Most recently, Kirk was chosen from more than 500 entries nationwide as a Territory Winner in the Sub-Zero contest.

Kirk's signature style combines varied heights and angles with multiple finishes, woods and paints. The result is a unique kitchen created with Heritage or Kennebec cabinetry.

KITCHENS UNIQUE BY LOIS, INC.

◄

Hand-rubbed cabinetry, hand-
carved corbels and valances, and a
hand-painted tile mural highlight
this upscale, almost formal,
kitchen.

▲

The lighting shelf above the island is adorned with hand-painted tiles of fruit and vegetables and casts both indirect and direct lighting. The open hutch displays dishes and collectibles.

◀

Kennebec's Old World craftsmanship complements today's lifestyle. A warm Shaker-style design with hand-hewed beams surrounds the most modern conveniences.

▶

A sculpted, country French valance shelf adds charm — and eliminates the need for art or wallpaper. The shelf's finish matches the cabinetry; its carvings duplicate a design on the range hood.

A National Kitchen and Bath Association Design Award winner, this kitchen — with its angles and two-tone finish — exemplifies the design signature of Kitchens Unique By Lois.

▼

LA Associates
4200 Aurora Street, Suite B
Coral Gables, FL 33146
P 305.444.8401 F 305.444.8405

Beryl Armstrong

Linda Lieber

Since it was founded in 1984, LA Associates has installed hundreds of luxury kitchens in the Southeastern United States, the Bahamas and South America.

Usually working in collaboration with architects and interior designers, we create kitchens that are beautiful, nurturing and comfortable, making them ideal environments for family and friends to come together and enjoy each other's company. Our rooms give precedence to cooking and eating, the primary activities around which we share and celebrate in the '90s.

We use the lifestyle and dreams of our clients as our guides. We have moved beyond the work triangle concept, once so central to kitchen design. We still begin with function as the foundation of every plan. Comfort, ambience and style flow naturally from designs that are highly personal, yet timeless.

LA Associates offers the finest in kitchen technology, from storage systems to finishes. Styling options range from space-age contemporary, to French and English country, to craftsman, to classic Georgian - along with most combinations in between.

Attention to detail and service are the trademarks of LA Associates. We want our clients' dreams to come true.

Designed for two parents who love to cook, this family kitchen provides a nurturing environment by making it easy for their children to do homework, watch TV or play games nearby. The contemporary country style was created in collaboration with Judi Male, ASID. Note the mixture of cabinet styles, woods and finishes.

▲

Created in collaboration with
Charles Pawley, AIA, this room
appears warm and inviting even
though it relies on relatively
cold materials like sleek
polyester, stainless steel,
and granite. Casual, elegant
entertaining is made even
more enjoyable by bringing
the outdoors in with a view of
the sky and sea during the
day and city lights at night.

The U-shape work area accommodates a husband-and-wife cooking team comfortably in a tight area. The butcher-block table behind the peninsula is a wonderful place for daily dining or for friends to have a glass of wine while dinner is being prepared. An interesting combination of craftsman-style wood cabinets, French country tile and granite rounds out the scene.

Created in collaboration with Armando Valdes, AIA, this kitchen boasts classic dark cherry cabinetry, stainless steel tile, and a blue-and-white checkered backsplash. The prominent international family that owns the home needs the commercial range for large formal dinners. A classic butler's pantry allows for serving and clean-up away from the food preparation area.

LaMantia Kitchen Design Studio
9100 Ogden Avenue
Brookfield, IL 60513
P 708.387.9900 F 708.485.2023

Joseph LaMantia, CKD

Lynn Larsen, CKD

Since 1974, LaMantia Kitchen Design Studio has developed an outstanding reputation in the design/build market. A team of certified kitchen designers, architects and project managers guides clients from the initial design concept through construction and installation.

The team's goal on each project is to create functional kitchens and additions that uniquely reflect the lifestyle of LaMantia's clients, while preserving the architectural integrity of their homes.

LaMantia's outstanding designs have earned national awards and recognition from manufacturers such as KitchenAid, Heritage Custom Kitchens and Crystal Cabinet Works.

The pride LaMantia takes in its work is ultimately transformed into the pride of ownership satisfied customers feel after their project is completed. Two Chicago-area showrooms display the company's ingenuity and commitment to craftsmanship and quality products.

LaMantia Kitchen
Design Studio

◀

Courtesy KitchenAid Major Appliances

A new bay window, skylights and softly angled cabinetry expand this award-winning kitchen. Hunter green and warm knotty pine accent the home's pastoral setting.

▲

Aesthetics and function meet in this kitchen of fine cherry and stainless steel. An expanded peninsula allows guests to congregate, yet separates them from the preparation, cooking and clean-up areas. The client's preference for red is reflected in the brick red cabinetry accents and backsplash tile.

 ▲

Herbs dry while homemade preserves cool in this functional storage area. An antique stove treasured by the client complements Shaker-detailed cabinetry and tile.

▶

Restrained detail, softened earth tones and the heavy grain of oak reflect the Arts and Crafts style of this home. A removable oak backsplash allows access to an existing low window.

The family room addition to this traditional home accommodates the many activities of a contemporary family. The carefully detailed cabinetry, plank flooring and fireplace amplify the client's collection of colonial antiques.

▶

Madison Design Group
1700 Stutz Drive, Suite 27
Troy, MI 48084
P 810.643.4770   F 810.643.9177

Janice Steinhardt
Gary Fried

Madison Design Group is a young, energetic design firm specializing in custom cabinetry for kitchens and baths. Only the finest American and European cabinetry is used for the discerning tastes of the firm's sophisticated clients. The philosophy of this small company is to provide unsurpassed personalized service while creating "classic, functional and exciting design solutions for the entire home."

Madison Design Group has been featured in a variety of national publications and has captured numerous awards for its use of innovative combinations of materials and its fresh designs. Located in the Michigan Design Center, the firm services the area's finest architects, designers, builders and contractors.

Classic raised-panel polyfoil doors reflect the sophistication of this elegant home. Open shelving and glass mullion doors allow the homeowner to display objets d'art. Glass cabinetry, a motorized pull-out pantry, and wine storage complete this functional, yet elegant design.

MADISON DESIGN GROUP

This lakefront kitchen with an angle on design is highlighted by blue pearl granite in an unusual geometric shape. This high-gloss laminate cabinetry is filled with custom drawers and swivel compartments, including a swing-out pantry, a desk area featuring "mini-cubbies," and glass doors for displaying collectibles. The glass cabinets over the wet bar provide an unobstructed view of the beautiful waterfront.

A dynamic island, reminiscent of a space capsule, is the focal point of this spectacular contemporary home in the country. Numerous skylights provide natural light that enhances the pewabic tile on the countertops. A specially designed maple mullion door and custom cabinet hardware are among the many innovations that make this kitchen unique.

Maple cabinetry and counter-tops of granite and ribbed stainless steel complement the natural surroundings of this bold, contemporary home. Two islands, one for food preparation and casual meals and the other a mini-wet bar for entertaining, are ideal for this young family's lifestyle.

▶

"Country Chic" describes this impeccably detailed kitchen. Massive turnings highlight the white beaded doors. Separate cooking and baking areas are enriched with beautiful crown moldings, plate racks and mullion glass doors.

"Residential high-tech" best describes this navy and black high-gloss laminate kitchen. The richness of the cabinets comple-ments the cool, ribbed, stainless steel work surfaces, while the oak flooring adds warmth. Built-in appliances contribute to the kitchen's sleek design and two built-in TVs make it a great place for gathering and entertaining.

▼

NDM Kitchens, Inc.
& Nancy Mullan's Kitchens
204 East 77th Street
New York, NY 10021
P 212.628.4629   F 212.628.6738

Four small rooms were combined to create this large, efficient space for a professional cook. Storage is maximized by hanging racks, roll-out shelves, "The Nancy Mullan signature step stool" in its own convenient slot, and lots of original glass-front wall cabinets stripped of years of paint.

◀

Nancy D. Mullan, ASID, CKD

The sleek, streamlined, "hardwareless" look of this kitchen is softened by the warm almond of the countertops, the pickled-oak floor, the walls and the stone of the alabaster lighting fixture, antique column used as a table base, and the outside terrace.

▶

Nancy Mullan is a Professional member of the American Society of Interior Designers, a Certified Kitchen Designer, and a licensed home-improvement contractor.

She has designed and installed hundreds of high-end kitchens, primarily in the New York metropolitan area, including Manhattan, Greenwich, Connecticut, and the Hamptons. She has worked elsewhere throughout the United States and as far afield as Lyford Cay in the Bahamas.

Mullan's work has been published in several books and numerous national publications, including *Country Living* (cover), *House Beautiful's Kitchens/Bath* (cover) and *Woman's Day* special publications. She is a regular participant in the most prestigious designer showhouses, such as Kips Bay, Southampton and Greenwich.

Among the products Mullan has enjoyed using recently are Armstrong flooring, Avonite countertops, KitchenAid appliances and Wood-Mode cabinets, all seen in the accompanying photographs.

Mullan designs her kitchens to encourage the novice, enhance the professional, and seduce family and friends. She undertakes each new project mindful of William Morris' timeless instruction to "have nothing in your houses that you do not know to be useful or believe to be beautiful."

NDM Kitchens, Inc.
& Nancy Mullan's Kitchens

Nancy Mullan used visual tricks here to make the space seem wider than its 6 1/2 feet. With elegant neoclassic motifs and hand-carved mahogany countertops and backsplashes, as well as an integrated refrigerator and 18" dishwasher, this kitchen proves that a tiny space can contain all the necessary equipment and still look great.

This kitchen was personalized with decorative paint, including a "carved" Latin inscription running around the top of the room that mentions the owners and their children, the designer, the carpenter, the painter and the date. It concludes with Horace's phrase, "Eheu fugace anni" (alas, the fleeting years).

▼

The beauty of real limestone and tumbled marble is combined here with the practicality of solid-surface "limestone" on the countertops. The lighting system is both dramatic and functional.

▲

The sink area is supremely functional, including an integral drainboard cut into the counter-top and a pull-out trash container. The radii on either side of the sink keep the room from looking like a tunnel and conceal dishtowels and a step stool. The handle of the sponge drawer doubles as a towel bar.

▶

Country Living featured this bright, cheerful kitchen on the cover of its July 1993 issue. The space was once dreary and oppressive. Mullan removed many of the dark wood cabinets, primed the remaining ones white, and washed them in blue. The "island" is a well-worn chopping block salvaged from a butcher's shop.

Decorative paint and soft, natural colors were used in this old farmhouse kitchen to create a soothing, timeless, ambience, as if the room had always looked just like this. To complete the feeling, the refrigerator masquerades as an antique armoire. But up-to-the-minute cabinets and appliances provide every modern convenience.

▶

nuHaus
1665 Old Skokie Road
Highland Park, IL 60035
P 708.831.1330   F 708.831.1377

Standing left to right: Bobbie Eiler, Jim Livingston, Marty Fahey, Doug Durbin (President), Lori Chazan, Kathleen Nelson, Kelly Nobles, Nancy Gordon

Sitting front left to right: Dawn Guildoo, Susan Brent, Dan Thiele

nuHaus is a unique company comprised of custom cabinetmakers, tile and stone craftsmen and custom contracting services. Its staff of 50 professionals operates out of an 8,000 square foot showroom on Chicago's North Shore, featuring a unique array of kitchen, bath and lifestyle displays.

nuHaus' principals have more than 75 years of combined experience in every aspect of kitchen and bath design, construction and remodeling. They have each been recognized by national awards from their peers, and their work has appeared in such publications as *Better Homes & Gardens, Architectural Digest, Audio-Video Interiors, Woman's Day* and the *Chicago Tribune*.

nuHaus features the world's finest custom cabinet lines, such as Downsview, Rutt and William Ohs, as well as maintaining its own custom cabinet making and millwork division, Exclusive Woodworking.

In addition to its cabinet offerings, nuHaus displays a wide selection of designer hardware, fixtures and appliances and is the exclusive "Chatelain" dealer for La Cornue - the legendary handcrafted French range of cooking products and "batterie de cuisine."

The name nuHaus was inspired by the Bauhaus collective of the 1920's. Bauhaus' guiding philosophy was that there should be no distinction between the creative quality of the arts and trade crafts. nuHaus believes that its clients deserve comprehensive and uncompromised service, technical resources and insight in designing environments which both reflect and express how they want to live.

Traditional? Contemporary? How about balanced and beautiful! The cabinetry features today's clean lines, but with classic molding. The pecan floor and Verdi granite countertops contribute warmth and brilliance. ▲

The subtle unity of the light fixtures and the bold statement of the columns make this a kitchen to marvel at as well as live in. (Portfolio Design Group, Architects)

◀

The warmth and beauty of French
Country design, pictured with this
"antique" English work table,
redefines the concept of kitchen
cabinetry as furniture.

▲

From the contoured stainless steel backsplash/organizer of the message center to the recessed granite between the sinks, the thoughtful, unexpected detailing of high quality materials characterizes this kitchen.

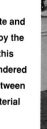

Sweeping curves of granite and pearwood invite us to enjoy the warmth and efficiency of this contemporary kitchen, rendered with a delicate balance between geometry and striking material combinations.

▶

Tucked into its own niche, the tailored efficiency of this kitchen desk area is expressed here in warm mocha tones on alderwood and capped in Rosa Girona marble.

▶

The marriage of efficiency and visual interest: thoughtful design allows the cook to take no more than a few steps in any direction to prepare and clean up after a meal. Meanwhile, changes in vertical planes and the juxtaposition of linear and curved elements create movement and excitement.

The cleanliness and balance of horizontal and vertical lines in contemporary design is demonstrated in this vignette from their showroom.

This handcrafted Tuscany-styled country kitchen offers a taste of the Old World: a warm gathering place where one imagines the cooking area as an updated hearth; where diverse finishes and textures, unfitted cupboards and cherished heirlooms combine with modern conveniences to create an environment of uncommon form, function and charm.

▼

Originally divided into three rooms, this kitchen/breakfast room/sitting area was blended into a single space. Its various functions are now differentiated by cased archways stained to match the cabinetry. Elegant traditional details and charmingly rustic finishes and textures work together to unify and personalize the environment.

The beauty of knotted pine is extended from this kitchen into the adjoining breakfast area where classic elegance and warm country informality are delicately mixed. The varied heights of the unusual island underscore its distinct functions - as informal breakfast bar, meal preparation area and message center. They also guarantee that meal preparation takes place largely out of sight of the breakfast and family room.

Details, details. Outside light streams through glass mullioned door cabinets that reflect and reinforce this home's airy architecture. Note also the subtle relationships between design details: the curvature of the countertop to the cased archways, for instance, and the valance pattern under the cabinets to the support bracket under the countertops. (Stuart Cohen and Julie Hacker Architects)

▲

Perched on the edge of a wooded ravine, this lovely master bath features an unusual lavatory peninsula that's functional and visually compelling. Contrasts in both the geometry and materials of this space create a unique and inviting haven. (Architecture: Stuart D. Shayman Associates)

▶

Polished limestone and marble reinforce the strength and elegance of this master bathroom. Classic balance is emphasized by beaded columns framing the washbasin and mirror. Note the built-in dresser on the right.

▲

Though large, this traditional white kitchen boasts a tight, efficient work pattern. Its signature arch motif, as seen on the custom range hood and open island cabinet, is borrowed from the English manor home's architectural millwork and stonework.

▼ ▶

Past Basket
200 South Third Street
Geneva, IL 60134
P 708.208.1011   F 708.208.1445

765 F Woodlake Road
Kohler, WI 53044
P 414.459.9976   F 414.459.9996

David McFadden

Past Basket was established in 1976 by Linda McFadden. Past Basket has evolved from a resource for fine antiques and home accessories to a company that now also creates custom kitchens. Departure from the ordinary and close attention to detail earn Past Basket the respect of clients, peers and national publications.

President Dave McFadden earned a degree in mechanical engineering from the University of Notre Dame. He spent 29 years, in industry, as a design engineer and as vice president of new product development for an international corporation.

Now as president and primary designer for Past Basket, he oversees the company's operations in Geneva, Illinois and Kohler, Wisconsin. Past Basket's proximity to Chicago and Milwaukee makes the company especially suited to serving clients in those two metropolitan areas.

Balanced physical proportion enables large ornate moldings and corbels to ease into the design. An alternative cooking center, although visually consistent with the whole kitchen, enjoys a certain sense of functional autonomy.

◀

PAST BASKET

◄

An inviting and functional
design is warmed through the
use of high-grade cherry
cabinets and soapstone
counters.

▲

Close examination of the "hutch end" reveals meticulous craftsmanship and a soothing relationship between the tumbled marble counter and cabinetry.

◀ ▼

Here, a feeling of fine furniture from a more primitive period is accomplished by using various natural materials. The island with a black "rub-through" finish and the wall cabinetry with white glaze on maple are complemented by the slate floor.

▲

Purdy's Design Studio
2101 Richmond Road
Beachwood, OH 44122
P 216.831.1520   F 216.831.1520*

William L. Purdy

Purdy's Design Studio has more than 25 years of experience creating and designing kitchens and baths. The company works with many architects and interior designers from its extensive showroom in Cleveland.

Owner Bill Purdy's philosophy that a well-designed kitchen must first be functional, stems from his architectural background.

He establishes a comfortable working relationship with his clients through a genuine personality and a wealth of product knowledge. A Purdy's kitchen is functional, elegant, creative and timeless — a style achieved through the use of high-quality American cabinetry hand crafted in the Old World manner.

Purdy is past president of the Ohio Chapter of the National Kitchen and Bath Association and a 1993 winner in the Heritage Kitchen Design Contest. His kitchens have appeared in publications such as *House Beautiful Home Remodeling, Kitchen & Bath Concepts* and *Cleveland Magazine.*

Purdy's Design Studio also focuses on entertainment units and clothing storage areas as two non-traditional areas of expertise, but the company feels the kitchen is the heart of any home. For many homeowners, kitchen remodeling is a once-in-a-lifetime event that can make a big difference in the quality of their lifestyle.

The right combination of materials and colors can make a kitchen come alive with excitement and style.

▼

Beauty combines with function to create a style that knows no boundaries. Note the distinctly personal look of the custom cabinetry.

▲

◀

Careful selection of lighting,
flooring and countertops, as
well as close attention to space
planning and color coordination,
results in a showcase kitchen.

▲

Living a life of luxury becomes much easier with a sophisticated, stylish bathroom.

◄ ▲ ►

Though engineered for maximum efficiency, this kitchen knows how to be beautiful, too - especially through its custom cabinetry.

◄ ▲▼

Putnam Kitchens, Inc.

Peter J. Genovese
Dana M. Clarrissimeaux
John D. Schlegel, P.K.B.P.

406 East Putnam Avenue
Cos Cob, CT 06807
P 203.661.2270 F 203.661.6637

Here, custom cherry cabinetry
with traditional door styling
complements solid-surface
countertops and backsplashes.
The commercial range is a
welcome feature for serious
chefs.

▲

Designers at Putnam Kitchens, Inc. have more than 75 years of combined experience in designing and installing high-end kitchens across the country. We have worked extensively in Greenwich, Connecticut; Beverly Hills, California; Newport, Rhode Island; New York City; and Florida.

Homeowners, architects and interior designers turn to us for expert advice in kitchen and bathroom planning.

We pride ourselves in designing environments that are functionally smart and aesthetically pleasing, while staying within the investment parameters of our clients.

PUTNAM KITCHENS, INC.

◄

The cabinets in this
contemporary kitchen feature a
metallic-lacquered, smoke-gray
finish. Note the black granite
and mirrored backsplash and
marble tile floor.

▲

Mornings begin pleasantly thanks to custom traditional cabinetry in white high-gloss lacquer styling. Distinctive contrast is provided by green marble countertops and backsplashes, along with a full-high mirrored backsplash.

▲

Handmade cabinetry beautifully interprets American Shaker styling. The blue finish matches an armoire in the family area.

Regency Kitchens & Custom Interiors
4204 14th Avenue
Brooklyn, NY 11219
P 718.435.4266 F 718.435.5411

Regency Kitchens & Custom Interiors is a family owned business which has produced award-winning kitchens for more than ten years. Their experience combining quality craftsmanship and superior design has brought them numerous awards, including a first place in the 1995 NKBA design competition.

"The kitchen should be a space with an aura, full of personality and warmth," says principal designer Rochelle Kalisch, who runs the business with her husband, Ruven (who serves as project manager). "My primary challenge is to figure out what inspires each client.

Though kitchens are the focus of Rochelle's profession, they're not her only canvas. A graduate of Parson's School of Interior Design, Rochelle is a multifaceted designer whose background includes calligraphy, illustration, oil painting, graphic design and art instruction.

Rochelle's philosophy is to pick out the positive and make it work.

"Like people, every space comes with its own personality and individual characteristics," she says. "When interviewing clients, I encourage them to express their wishes. Often, they feel their wish list is too extensive for the limited space they have. My greatest reward is to see the joy on their face when they receive more than they expected.

"I believe in getting to know my clients on a personal level. That is the only way to learn what elements will evoke the right mood for them."

Regarding design in general, Rochelle allows that the process can be extremely detailed and complex.

"Nevertheless," she says, "it should be an exciting journey filled with much learning, anticipation and enjoyment that will last long after the project has been completed."

Rochelle Kalisch

REGENCY KITCHENS
& CUSTOM INTERIORS

◄

Sleek and contemporary, with a
touch of tradition, this kitchen is
highly efficient, featuring a
bi-level island that allows for
plenty of circulation.

▲

An octagon island rises from alternating strips of natural oak in contrasting stains to become the core of a busy kitchen.

▲

Here, a French country hood and lowered cooking area serve as an attractive focal point.

▲

Traditional styling of beaded inset, raised-panel doors blends with granite countertops and backsplash. Note the charming display cabinets over the peninsula.

◄

Playroom shelves keep toys organized, while allowing visual access from the kitchen for child supervision. ◄

Angled display shelves, capped with a detailed crown molding, frame this window. ◄

Open counter areas and a see-through cabinet enclose this kitchen while integrating a view of the outdoors into the decor. A watchful eye can be kept on children in the play area during meal preparation. ▲

Contemporary styling commands attention. Contrasting elements create a dramatic touch, while the curve of the counters is echoed in the cabinets above. Note how the counter wraps around to form a breakfast/snack area. ◄

Rutt of New York City
George Rallis
150 East 58th Street
New York, NY 10155
P 212.752.7888   F 212.644.2086

The wonderful diversity of Rutt cabinetry is exemplified by these custom solid cherry panels in a library setting.

◄

George Rallis

George Rallis earned his bachelor's and master's degrees in architecture from Pratt Institute and has been working in interior design and construction for more than 20 years. With his partner, Alyson Fadini, and a highly professional, experienced staff with AIA, ASID and CKD credentials, he has created Rutt of New York.

Rutt custom cabinets have been built in Lancaster, PA, for more than 40 years. Still 100% custom, Rutt remains America's last uncompromising cabinet maker. A diverse selection of styles and finishes enhances any living environment.

The designer's ability to convey the client's personal design statement is crucial. Since no cabinets in America are built with such exacting adherence to their specifications, the construction and finishing of Rutt cabinets is an art form. They have often been copied, but never equaled. Classic styles like Georgetown, a Rutt original, have helped set the pace for home design for years.

Rutt of New York maintains a 4,000-square-foot showroom in the Architects and Designers Building. It showcases superb examples of cabinetry crafted with attention to detail and respect to timeless, elegant design.

◀

An original Shaker design by Rallis
showcases distressed pine
cabinetry. The custom tile is from
Country Floors. Note the 300-year-
old planks used for countertops,
the barn siding for backsplashes,
the English tub sink and the
tumbled marble floor.

▲

This American Renaissance kitchen incorporates Georgian, Colonial, Victorian, Deco and Shaker style details with Arts and Crafts tile by Country Floors. An eclectic style for a discriminating client, it's one of Rallis' original designs for Rutt.

This kitchen reflects Rallis' interpretation of the unfitted English style with natural maple cabinetry, Mexican tile floors, Corian counters and hand-painted tile backsplashes.

Rallis used many angles in this sophisticated contemporary kitchen with cherry cabinetry. The angles increase the amount of cabinetry and countertop space and elevate the kitchen to an art form.

Here, Rallis collaborated with architect Nathan Bibliowitz to create a warm country kitchen with natural cherry and custom tile.

This sleek contemporary design houses a 36" television, stereo equipment, desk area and bookcases. The cherry and black round columns are reminiscent of Deco style cabinetry.

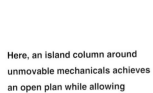

Here, an island column around unmovable mechanicals achieves an open plan while allowing separate areas for cooking and living space. The cabinets are solid wood with a baked enamel finish. Featured are Corian and granite countertops.

St. Charles of New York
150 East 58th Street
New York, NY 10155
P 212.838.2812   F 212.308.4951

The designers at St. Charles of New York combine over 140 years of professional experience in kitchen design. We create distinctive environments that meet the needs and desires of our clients. Our vast product offering reaches all ends of the spectrum - from steel to custom wood-frame, to laminate and polyester. We are proud to declare that we can provide whatever our clients want.

Old World elegance is achieved in this kitchen through the classic combination of hand-hewn decorative beams and washed oak cabinets.

Fine furniture elements are featured in the fluted pilasters on the island and the exquisite details of the hood.

St. Charles of New York

A vintage green island with a rich butcher block work surface accents natural bamboo cherry wood cabinets. The warm Juparana Vayara granite countertops combine with eclectic, colorful accessories to create an inviting country kitchen in the city.

Washed pine softens stainless steel and glass cabinetry in this versatile kitchen. Note the distinctive sink cabinet reminiscent of old-fashioned English Country sinks and crafted from rich verde granite.

 ▶

An efficient cooking kitchen doubles as a comfortable family center in this 1993 Kips Bay Designer Showhouse. The chameleon properties of stainless steel cabinetry reflect the warm earth tones of the tumbled marble backsplash and floor. Interior design by Gail Green, Ltd.

The challenge in this 1994 Kips Bay Designer Showhouse was to design a functional room within a limited space. Sleek copper-colored cherry wood cabinets, absolute black granite countertops, and space-enhancing mirror backsplashes create a sophisticated, handsome kitchen. Interior design by Billy W. Francis Design/Decoration.

Shields & Company
43 East 78th Street
New York, NY 10021
P 212.794.4455   F 212.794.3881

This rustic Western-style kitchen can be found in a beach house on an island in the Atlantic Ocean.

Gail Shields-Miller

Shields & Company, a multifaceted interior design firm established in 1960, is comfortable in both commercial and residential markets. Under the leadership of Gail Shields-Miller, the firm has designed numerous kitchens and baths, as well as complete renovation projects, throughout the Northeast, Southeast and the Bahamas.

Several of these elegant kitchens and baths have been highlighted in various design publications, including *Showcase of Interior Design*. One was featured on the cover of *Interior Decorators' Handbook*.

The company's philosophy is that the kitchen has become the focal point of family living in the 90's and, therefore, must serve a variety of purposes. Each project takes into account family size, lifestyle, practicality and comfort, as well as technical advances in the field.

Working with superior craftspeople and providing attention to detail, Shields & Company feels each project must satisfy the needs of the client and the aesthetic dimensions of the space. A balance must be reached among color, materials, lighting, and architectural details to achieve the elegance and timelessness of good design - with the emphasis clearly on function.

SHIELDS & COMPANY

◀

**The glass gazebo dinette area
of this kitchen is offset by
high-tech lighting, "buttery"
beige cabinets and glass block.**

▲

Crisp white lacquered cabinets are
juxtaposed against classic
Chippendale-style chairs in this
elegant country house.

▲

The warm tones of the custom wood cabinetry are mimicked in the painted ceiling and Italian tile floors for a peaceful monochromatic look.

Thanks to a raised ceiling in the work area and the addition of three skylights with suspended lighting, this kitchen offers a feeling of extra space.

The black granite kitchen table is suspended off the cabinetry and balanced by an angled steel column, allowing for extended counter surface or casual dining.

Thurston Kitchen & Bath
2920 East 6th Avenue
Denver, CO 80206
P 303.399.4564

For almost two decades, the designers at Thurston Kitchen & Bath, Inc. have been designing custom kitchens and baths in Colorado and beyond. Our more than fifty designers have added dimension of function, style and beauty to thousands of homes, condominiums and townhomes.

Based on a philosophy of mutual respect, our designers work closely with clients during the entire design process, from concept to installation. By managing the elements of form, function, detail, color, textures, patterns and light, we create a living space that features timeless design reflecting personal taste. No matter how discriminating, or the number of special wants and needs, we have the experience, desire and quality products and craftsmanship to make our clients' dreams a reality.

Our showrooms are located in Aspen, Boulder, Breckenridge, Crested Butte, Denver, Ridgway, Steamboat Springs, Telluride and Vail, as well as the SieMatic/ Smallbone Showroom at the Denver Design Center. As we say in the West, we know the territory.

The crackle finish on this custom-made centerpiece creates an antique look and feel. Note the large spaces for storing and displaying favorite objects. Boulder, Colorado.

▲

Thurston Kitchen & Bath

Large open-cut log walls create a feeling of permanence and the West. The interior boasts a comfortable feel, echoed within the design of the kitchen. The cabinets are clear vertical grain fir in a natural finish. Unique marble-top island and AGA range enhance the function and style. Telluride, Colorado.

Here, sleek design is accented with a Southwestern flair. The older cabinets feature an autumn red heirloom finish. Reflections of light bounce from the absolute black granite tile countertops. Eagle, Colorado.

The clean, airy design and functional layout provide maximum open space and room to move. The island offers extra workspace and style. Eagle, Colorado.

Clean lines and track lighting create a warm, inviting atmosphere. The Vulcan range provides a commercial touch. Note also the Fountainhead countertops and oak cabinets with cherry stain. Crested Butte, Colorado.

▶

Traditional lines accent classic cabinet design in medium stain on butternut. The countertops are venziano granite. Vail, Colorado.

▲

This spacious kitchen makes it easy to prepare food and accommodate large gatherings. The stainless steel hood and Viking range incorporate commercial touches. Vail, Colorado.

▶

Recipes For Total Satisfaction From The Great Kitchen Designers

Imagine an opportunity to talk with some of the country's top kitchen experts about their own habits in "the gathering place of the nineties." Who better to provide tips and share philosophies on the use of a kitchen? Kitchen designers look into the lives of hundreds of clients, allowing them to learn what works and what doesn't in their own space.

The following section is a collection of ideas, hints and recipes. Some designers shared traditions that have been in their family for generations; others chose to include dishes which reflect their lifestyle and philosophy of design.

We found that the designers' lives reflect those of most of us; they enjoy entertaining often in a simple, elegant manner, and most prepare meals with a gathering of friends or relatives. Because of their thriving businesses, many of the experts save cooking for a weekend activity, but a few still prepare a sit-down meal nearly every night.

Whatever their preference, designers' expertise in the kitchen extends to the culinary as well as the functional aspects of the space. From salad dressing to Cornish game hen, we have gathered a sumptuous selection of dishes and helpful ideas from the top talent in the country. Enjoy!

Pirrie B. Aves

bulthaup (LA) Inc : The bulthaup extractor removes cooking steam and water vapor. The glass shelf provides convenient access to spices and ingredients. Also, note how utensils can be hung on the rail.

▲

American Classic Kitchens, Inc.
Anna Mesaikos

Anna Mesaikos claims she "became more Greek" when she married her husband George. He came to the United States from Greece as a furrier and, according to Anna, he is a creative and talented cook. "I cook, too, but I have to have everything laid out in front of me," Anna explains. "Cooking for a party larger than four intimidates me, but my husband is comfortable preparing food for large groups because of his experience in the restaurant business."

The couple often entertains family and friends. "It's in our blood," asserts Anna. "Greeks don't just sit down for a drink, we share mezedakia (Greek appetizers). Mediterranean people are very warm and lively."

Along with representing the designer's heritage, the spinach with rice and the tzatziki are light and delicious. According to Mesaikos, the tzatziki is on the Greek table at all times, and the spinach with rice is "a creative way to get children to eat spinach." Her eight- and ten-year-old girls not only enjoy eating the meal, they also love to help prepare the food. Mesaikos suggests serving the spinach with rice as a side dish or an entrée in the summer.

"In the Greek culture," says Mesaikos, "you make us happy if you eat. That attitude is handed down from generation to generation, and therefore the kitchen is a very important space to us. We cook with our children, and we entertain out of the kitchen."

SPINACH WITH RICE
serves 4-6
2 large onions, finely chopped
3/4 cup olive oil
1 teaspoon tomato paste
1 pound spinach or 2 packages frozen spinach
1 cup water
1/2 cup raw rice
fresh mint
salt and pepper

Sauté onions in olive oil until soft; add tomato paste and spinach and stir. Add enough water to cover spinach. Bring to a boil; add seasonings and mint. Sprinkle rice on top. Do not stir. Cover and simmer until the rice is cooked.

TZATZIKI (Greek Yogurt Sauce)
This sauce is always on the Greek table. We use it as a dip for vegetables and pita bread, or as a sauce for fish, meat, gyros or sandwiches. It can even be used as a salad dressing. Be creative!

1 cup yogurt
1/2 coarsely grated cucumber
2 teaspoons olive oil
1 teaspoon white wine vinegar
1 garlic clove
2 teaspoons fresh dill
salt and pepper to taste

Mix all ingredients together. Serve.

DeWitt Talmadge Beall: Waste and recycling containers located beneath the butcher's block introduce an extra level of functionality. White cabinetry beautifully frames the flowers inside and out.

▲

ANNE K. DONAHUE INTERIOR DESIGN
Anne Donahue

After 11 years in the kitchen design business working for others, Anne has run her own kitchen design business since 1992.

In the diverse Los Angeles area, she has worked for clients from many cultural backgrounds with varied culinary practices. She has designed for Japanese clients, for Chinese clients, for clients who want kosher kitchens, and for clients who want commercial kitchens. "Each client has a different vision and need for the use of space", she says.

When Anne and her husband, Robert, designed and built their own Hollywood Hills home with architect William Wietsma, they included a fabulous Siematic kitchen. Anne loves cooking in her kitchen, which includes a baking space and a Gaggenau convection oven, "great for baking and roasting." It also includes two work areas and a cleanup area.

The Donahues love to entertain. On Friday nights, they frequently invite guests over for a lovely Sabbath meal. Preparation is an important part of the Jewish Sabbath. Candles are lit on the dining room table. Kosher wine and challah (bread) are served as the spiritual part of the meal. Fresh flowers and the best china and silver are also included. With these physical preparations comes a psychological readiness, because the Sabbath is also a state of mind.

With a new baby at her home and her love of cooking and entertaining, Anne spends a great deal of time in her kitchen.

"Every kitchen needs to be designed around the client," she says. "The space is unique because it is used by everyone, all the time."

After a hectic stress-filled week in a big city like Los Angeles, there is one 6000 year-old tradition our family and friends still like to enjoy: a Friday night Sabbath meal.

The following is an example of a menu I use. Generally, we invite our family as well as our neighbors and friends. Each week we switch off to a different family's home.

Menu for 8 People:
Chilled Persian Carrot Soup
Roast Garlic Chicken
Basmati Rice with Asparagus and Vidalia Onions
Raisin Challah
Mixed Green Salad with Balsamic Vinaigrette
Yardin Chardonnay
Michel Richard's Halvah-Chocolate Mousse Napoleon (Parve)
Sumatra Coffee

CHILLED PERSIAN CARROT SOUP
4 teaspoons vegetable oil
8 onions, chopped
6 garlic cloves, minced
2 eggplants, peeled, seeded and diced
4 tablespoons chopped parsley
16 cups water
2 ribs celery, chopped
16 large carrots, peeled and chopped
4 potatoes, peeled and chopped
3 teaspoons salt, plus more to taste
4 teaspoons freshly ground pepper, plus more to taste
4 teaspoons chopped fresh mint

Heat oil in a large, heavy non-reactive pot over medium heat. Cook onion and garlic for 5 minutes. Stir in eggplant and parsley and cook until softened, about 10 minutes. Add 16 cups of water, celery, carrots and potatoes. Simmer for 15 minutes. Stir in salt and pepper and cook over low heat for 30 minutes. Let cool.

In batches, purée the soup in a food processor. Refrigerate until cold. Season with salt and pepper to taste, divide among 8 bowls, garnish with mint and serve immediately.

ROAST GARLIC CHICKEN
1 7-pound chicken
3 teaspoons salt
freshly ground pepper to taste
8 sprigs fresh thyme
8 garlic cloves, peeled and lightly crushed

To make the chicken: the day before serving, sprinkle the chicken with salt and pepper. Place the sprigs of thyme and the garlic in the chicken by running your fingers between the skin and the flesh over the breast and legs to create pockets to insert the garlic and thyme. Wrap in plastic and refrigerate overnight.

DeWitt Talmadge Beall: Spice rack swings out independently from the door. Spices are stored on both sides of the swingout, thus doubling storage space.

▲

Preheat oven to 350 degrees. I use a Gaggenau convection oven with a meat thermometer, which helps make the chicken moist. I place the chicken on a simple rack uncovered. The hot air convection oven circulates air completely around the chicken, creating a pocket of air which keeps the juices in and leaves it brown and crispy on the outside. The cooking time for this oven is about 1 hour and 20 minutes, but with the meat thermometer, I set the internal temperature for 165 degrees.

BASMATI RICE WITH ASPARAGUS AND VIDALIA ONIONS
(The New York Times)
3 cups basmati rice
6 cups chicken stock or broth
5 cups chopped vidalia onion
4 teaspoons toasted sesame oil
36 medium asparagus
12 sprigs mint
1/2 teaspoon salt

Wash rice thoroughly. Combine with stock and bring to a boil in a large heavy-bottom pot.

Heat oil in a non-stick pan. When oil is hot, add chopped onions, reduce heat to medium high and sauté onion until it softens and begins to brown. When rice begins to boil, reduce to simmer and cover, cooking a total of 17 minutes.

Wash and break tough stems from asparagus at the point where the woody part meets the tender part. Cut the asparagus just below the head and then cut remaining stems into 1-inch pieces. When onion is soft, stir into the rice. Place a steamer in the pot in which the onion was cooked and place asparagus in the steamer; cook about 3 minutes, until the asparagus is tender but crisp.

Wash, dry and mince enough mint to make 5 tablespoons. When rice is cooked, stir in drained asparagus and add mint and salt.

RAISIN CHALLAH
yields 6 loaves or 4 loaves and 12 rolls
4 cups warm water
2 tablespoons dry yeast
4 eggs
1/2 cup oil
1/2 cup honey
2 cups raisins (or less, to taste)
14-15 cups flour
1 tablespoon coarse kosher salt

Glaze:
1 egg, beaten
poppy seeds

Pour warm water into a large mixing bowl. Stir in yeast, add eggs, oil, honey and raisins. Mix well and add about half of the flour. Stir well.

Let mixture rest 45 minutes to 1 hour until the yeast is bubbly. This is the first rising.

Add salt and most of the remaining flour. Mix and knead on a lightly floured board, adding only as much flour as necessary to be able to handle the dough. The dough should be soft. You may let the dough rise again for 1 hour, if desired.

Separate challah with a blessing. Divide dough, and shape loaves or rolls. Place challah in greased loaf pans or baking sheets and let rise 45 minutes to 1 hour.

Preheat oven to 350 degrees. Brush tops of loaves or rolls with beaten egg and sprinkle with poppy seeds. Bake for about 45 minutes to 1 hour for loaves, or 30 minutes for rolls. Remove from pans and cool on racks.

MIXED GREEN SALAD
12 cups assorted baby greens including arugala, radicchio, baby spinach, frisee and baby mustard greens
6-8 Roma tomatoes, quartered
3 scallions sliced horizontally 1/4 inch thick

DeWitt Talmadge Beall: French doors leading to an outside patio give this kitchen one more reason for being the center of family activity.

▲

BALSAMIC VINAIGRETTE
1/4 cup balsamic vinegar
1 tablespoon creamy Dijon-style mustard
1/4 teaspoon white pepper
1 teaspoon herbs of Provence
3/4 cup olive oil

In a mixing bowl, stir together mustard, pepper and herbs. Whisking continuously, very slowly pour in oil until blended.

Toss together dressing with mixed green salad ingredients; serve immediately.

MICHEL RICHARD'S HALVAH-CHOCOLATE MOUSSE NAPOLEAN
makes two 3x7 molds
12 ounces semi-sweet chocolate
1/2 pound unsalted margarine at room temperature
juice of 1/2 lemon
4 egg whites
2 tablespoons sugar
1 pound halvah, cut into 1/2-inch thick slices to fit molds
fresh mint leaves and strawberries for garnish
chocolate sauce (recipe follows)

Melt the chocolate in the top of a double boiler over simmering water. Let it cool to room temperature.

In the large bowl of an electric mixer with a whisk attachment, beat the chocolate and margarine until light and fluffy. Add the lemon juice and beat it in. In another bowl, beat the egg whites until soft peaks form, add sugar, and beat until stiff but not dry. Fold into the chocolate mixture. Spoon the chocolate mixture into a pastry bag fitted with a plain round tip.

Line 2 3x7 molds with parchment paper, allowing enough of it to hang over the edges so you can completely enclose the finished dessert. Carefully arrange slices of halvah to cover the entire bottom of each mold. Pipe a single layer of chocolate mousse about 1/2-inch thick over the halvah and then cover with another layer of halvah. Pipe a second layer of mousse and add another layer of halvah until you have 3 layers of halvah and 2 of mousse. Cover with the parchment paper and refrigerate for at least 2 hours.

About 30 minutes before serving, remove the dessert from the refrigerator. Invert the mold, releasing the paper-lined dessert; peel off the paper. Cut the mousse into 1-inch slices, dipping a sharp knife into hot water between the slices. Place on chilled dessert plates, cover with plastic wrap, and refrigerate. Just before serving, spoon chocolate sauce on one side of the mousse. Garnish with a mint leaf and fresh strawberries.

CHOCOLATE SAUCE
yields about 1 cup
8 ounces semi-sweet chocolate, coarsely chopped
1/2 cup strong hot coffee
1/2 cup apricot or strawberry preserves, strained
1 tablespoon fruit liqueur (optional)

In top of double boiler over simmering water, place chocolate, coffee, preserves and liqueur. Stir constantly until well blended. Transfer to glass bowl and cover with plastic. Can be served hot or chilled.

Bartcrest
Maureen Lennon

"Unlike most of my friends," says Maureen Lennon, "I prepare a meal every night. I cook often because I like to do it."

"People tend to be more casual today than they were years ago," she comments, but adds that she still prepares elegant dishes for entertaining. "*Elegant* does not necessarily mean *complicated*."

Lennon recognizes that guests like to feel "fussed over" with special desserts like her raspberry soufflé. "The dish is dramatic to present because everyone thinks it's

DeWitt Talmadge Beall: What better place to store cookbooks than above the range? Here, a conveniently located shelf keeps favorite recipes within easy reach.
◄

difficult to prepare and it looks gorgeous. And of course it tastes delicious," says Lennon, who also confides that the dish is really not difficult at all. Lennon advises that the only trick in preparing the soufflé is making certain no egg yolks get into the whites.

Lennon welcomes guests and family into her kitchen when she is preparing food. She remarks, "Today we are seeing more and more kitchen centers where Dad can join in, the kids can participate, and anyone else visiting the home can sit at the counter and be part of putting together a meal. The kitchen has become very much a focal point of the household."

RASPBERRY SOUFFLÉ
serves 4
1-1/4 cups puréed and sieved fresh or thawed frozen raspberries
3 tablespoons Chambord or other raspberry liqueur
5 egg whites
1/4 cup super fine sugar, plus extra for dusting dish
oil for soufflé dish

Preheat oven to 375 degrees. Using a 7-inch soufflé dish, wrap a double layer of wax paper or foil around the outside of the dish extending 2 inches above the rim. Tie in place to secure, brush dish and paper/foil with oil and dust with sugar.

Purée berries in food processor and add liqueur. Beat egg whites until they form stiff peaks, then beat in sugar until stiff and glossy. Carefully fold berry purée into egg whites.

Pour mixture into soufflé dish and level the top. Make a deep groove around the top about 1/2 inch from rim using the handle of a spoon. This will create a "top hat" effect when cooking.

Bake 30-35 minutes until soufflé is firm and doesn't wobble when shaken. Remove foil/paper and sprinkle with sifted confectioners' sugar (optional). Serve each portion with a serving of whipped cream, a few fresh raspberries and a sprig of mint.

DeWitt Talmadge Beall

DeWitt Talmadge Beall's self-described cooking style is "rough and ready." Beall claims his wife, Elina Katsioula, is the real creative genius of the kitchen. He enjoys learning culinary artistry by helping her.

Beall's menu is the creation of long-time friend and associate, chef Roger Kintz. Kintz has demonstrated cooking techniques and served as a consultant for Beall. Says Beall, "Since the kitchen is a tool that can work for or against you, I try to understand the problems of the cook."

"Today's kitchens tend to be expansive," he remarks. "But if the space isn't designed efficiently, that may mean you simply have more rope to hang yourself. If the area isn't designed to work, you may end up with an obstacle course."

To avoid the latter, Beall studies each kitchen in steps, looking at the parts of a process and the number of physical steps needed to complete a task. Beall has designed kitchen suites where a series of rooms center around the kitchen area. Some of his clients have eschewed dining rooms in favor of morning rooms, entertainment areas or offices off the kitchen.

When designing his own kitchen as well as those of his clients, Beall poses the question, "Can you do simple things simply and can you expand to do more complicated tasks?" In the Beall household, he explains, "You have to be able to bake a potato or prepare a meal for one hundred guests."

Menu:
Asian Mushroom Dumplings
Fire Roasted Red Pepper Soup
Grilled Chilean Sea Bass with Tumbleweeds of Leek-Roasted Root Vegetables
Wild Berry and Ginger Peach Crumble

ASIAN MUSHROOM DUMPLINGS
serves 4
This delightful appetizer is very simple to prepare and is virtually oil and fat free. Any mushroom may be substituted for this dish, but the selected varieties have a distinct flavor.

1 package won ton wrappers
6 ounces shitake mushrooms
6 ounces oyster mushrooms
1 bunch green onions
rice wine vinegar
1 tablespoon cornstarch
1 tablespoon extra virgin olive oil

Sauce:
1 bunch watercress or parsley
1 teaspoon Indonesian chile sauce (Oelek Sambal)
1 tablespoon lemon juice
1 garlic clove
1 tablespoon non-fat plain yogurt
1/4 teaspoon fresh ginger

Finely grind mushrooms and garlic in a food processor. Slice onions finely. Sauté both ingredients lightly and allow to cool. Lay out wrappers on a counter and place 1 teaspoon of mixture in center of wrapper. Fold in half and seal edges with mixture of cornstarch and water. Fold outside edges together to make a curved shape.

Place dumplings in a pot of boiling water and cook until translucent. Toss lightly with pesto and serve with skewers.

Sauce:
Purée all ingredients together in a food processor, adding the parsley or watercress first and slowly adding liquid ingredients until desired consistency is reached.

FIRE ROASTED RED PEPPER SOUP
serves 4
4 medium red bell peppers
1 tablespoon olive oil
1 clove garlic
2 medium red rose potatoes
3 tablespoons Mrs. Gooch's vegetarian chicken stock base
1 red onion
1 tablespoon chopped basil
1 teaspoon chopped sage
3-1/2 cups water or vegetable stock
1/2 cup tomato juice
1 tablespoon balsamic vinegar
pinch cayenne pepper
feta cheese for garnish

Using an open flame from the stove burners, hold peppers over the flame until the skin slightly bubbles and blackens uniformly. Place peppers in a paper or plastic bag, and allow to cool for 15 minutes.

Meanwhile, sauté onions, garlic and herbs lightly with olive oil. Add diced potatoes with skin on and continue cooking. Add all liquid ingredients and simmer 15 minutes.

Peel, seed and quarter the cooled peppers. Add these to the soup and cook for 5 minutes. Purée soup in a processor or blender and return to pan for a few minutes. Garnish with chopped herbs and crumbled feta cheese.

GRILLED CHILEAN SEA BASS WITH TUMBLEWEEDS OF LEEK
serves 4
This Southwestern dish is a fish lover's delight. The flaky texture of the fish combined with the nutritious red kale makes a healthy and unique combination that uses no oil or dairy products.

4 6-ounce portions of Chilean sea bass
2 bunches red kale
1 leek
lemon juice
1 teaspoon rice wine vinegar
salt and pepper to taste

Finely slice the white part of the leek lengthwise and bake in the oven for 40 minutes at 375 degrees.

Marinate the fish with lemon juice and cracked pepper. Grill or cook under a broiler for 8 minutes until cooked.

Wash and shred kale leaves finely. Place in a skillet with garlic and cook lightly with rice wine vinegar and natural juices only.

To serve: place kale on a plate, cooked fish on kale and tumbleweeds of leek on fish.

DIALOGUE OF ROASTED VEGETABLES
serves 4
This dish makes the most beautiful array of vegetables that will even stimulate the appetite of those who often avoid vegetables.

6 ounces mushrooms	1 bunch beets
5 violine onions	1 bunch baby carrots
1 yam	1/2 bunch green onions
1 zucchini (green or yellow)	4 small baby red rose potatoes
1 rutabaga	

bulthaup (LA) Inc: Two large, deep basins provide plenty of room for washing salads, vegetables or fruit. A sliding workboard brings prepared food above the basin — or the bowls that could be placed inside.

Marinade:
1 garlic clove
1/4 cup balsamic vinegar
1/4 cup extra virgin olive oil
1/2 teaspoon stone ground mustard
1 juiced lemon
1 sprig each of tarragon and basil
1/2 cup vegetable stock
salt and pepper to taste

Peel, cut into small pieces and blanch beets, rutabagas, potatoes, carrots and onions. Clean and cut remaining vegetables into small pieces. Combine ingredients for the marinade in a blender and purée. Pour marinade over vegetables and let stand for 1 hour.

   Place in a roasting pan and cook at 450 degrees for 30 minutes or until crispy.

INDIVIDUAL WILD BERRY AND GINGER PEACH CRUMBLE
serves 4
1 basket each of strawberries, raspberries, blackberries and other seasonal varieties.
Total of 4 baskets should be used.
6 peaches
1/2 cup Turbino or unrefined brown sugar
1/2 teaspoon vanilla bean extract
1/2 teaspoon powdered ginger
1 teaspoon cinnamon
pinch of nutmeg and allspice
4 tablespoons butter
1/3 cup pure maple syrup
1/2 cup unbleached whole wheat flour
1/3 cup chopped pecans
4 small white soufflé dishes

Clean fruit and slice peaches, leaving the skin on. Place fruit, ginger, sugar, vanilla and cinnamon in a small pot and bring to a simmer.

   Mix flour, sugar, spices, maple syrup, butter and chopped nuts together to form a crumble mixture.

   Divide lightly cooked fruit mixture between the 4 dishes. Cover with crumble mixture evenly on top and bake 15 minutes at 400 degrees until crumble is golden brown. Serve immediately.

BENVENUTI AND STEIN, INC.
Geno Benvenuti

Simplicity is a guiding philosophy in Geno Benvenuti's household. He chose his chicken primavera because it is "light and easy to prepare ... you only need to use one pan." As he does with all of his meal creations, Benvenuti developed this pasta dish on his own, adding or subtracting as he went along. He says, "The special touch is the sun-dried tomatoes."

Benvenuti & Stein, Inc.:
The beauty of natural wood
grain is emphasized
throughout this kitchen, even
in the matching refrigerator.

▲

Benvenuti hails from the Abruzzi region in Italy, where "the food is the best." The chefs in the region use their fingers to measure rather than spoons or cups. "My mother is a wonderful cook, which I didn't realize until I left home and my friends still went over to the house to eat," says Benvenuti.

"Usually I serve the chicken primavera on special occasions." Benvenuti slices the vegetables in advance so that he can prepare the dish at his kitchen's island while his guests gather around to watch and talk. Because the primavera is nearly a complete meal in itself, Benvenuti usually serves it with good bread and a bottle of Pinot Griggio. He contends that his wife makes an excellent salad as well.

Like most of his clients, Benvenuti and his family cook approximately once a week and on weekends. His children —ages two and seven — like to sit at the kitchen's island to watch and play while Benvenuti and his wife cook. He asserts, "Kitchens today have become the center of the first floor."

CHICKEN PRIMAVERA ALA GENO
serves 6-8
This is one of my favorite dishes to prepare while guests are watching. It is very easy for one person to do as long as all the ingredients are pre-cut and measured.

8 boneless/skinless chicken breasts, flattened
1/3 cup finely chopped sun-dried tomatoes
1 medium red bell pepper cut into long thin slices
1 medium green bell pepper cut into long thin slices
1 medium onion, thinly sliced
1 garlic clove, minced
1-1/2 cups favorite mushrooms, thinly sliced
1 cup slivered or thinly cut carrots
2 cups broccoli crowns
1/3 cup chopped parsley
4 ounces imported freshly grated Parmesan cheese
2/3 cup dry white wine
10 ounces chicken broth
6 ounces 2 percent milk
1/4 teaspoon freshly grated nutmeg or 1/2 teaspoon nutmeg powder
3 tablespoons olive oil
1/2 cup flour seasoned with salt and pepper
3 tablespoons butter
1 pound favorite twirling pasta ala dente
1 1/2 tablespoons cornstarch liquefied in 1/4 cup of water

In a large skillet, warm olive oil on medium heat, season with minced garlic.

DeWitt Talmadge Beall:
Blue accents on the tile and decorative plates enhance the air of perennial springtime in this bright kitchen.

▲

Lightly flour the chicken breasts on both sides and sear. Add the sun-dried tomatoes and turn the breasts. After 1 additional minute, add the wine and deglaze the pan. Remove the chicken and sauce completely. Keep warm.

In the skillet, melt butter and lightly sauté the peppers, onions, garlic, carrots, mushrooms and broccoli (add salt and pepper to taste). Next, add the chicken broth and milk, then add the Parmesan cheese and grated nutmeg over the mixture.

Move vegetables to the side and add liquefied cornstarch until it reaches desired consistency. Mix the chicken and the deglaze back into the skillet and simmer together for 6 minutes.

While this is simmering...
The pasta should be cooked, strained and placed into a large, flat serving dish. Remove the chicken to the side, take the vegetables and sauce and toss with the pasta. Then arrange the breasts on top. Sprinkle the parsley over the entire dish and serve.

BULTHAUP
Chris Tosdevin

Having installed kitchens from Singapore to Nigeria, and recently emigrated from England, Chris Tosdevin truly has an international perspective of kitchen design. "I have dealt with many different food cultures, and I find that aspect of my work fascinating," Tosdevin says. He adds that, even after 12 years in the business, he is still learning.

In his own kitchen, Tosdevin and his wife share the cooking duties and entertain often. "I like cooking because, like design, it is based on logic with regard to ingredients and proportions. I adjust flavorings according to people's tastes."   Usually Tosdevin cooks the entrée or dessert while he helps care for the couple's two young children.

"I like to invite guests into the kitchen when we are entertaining," says Tosdevin. He inevitably designs his own kitchens with extra space for multiple cooks and an area where guests can linger "without getting in the way."

Tosdevin sees the kitchen being very much integrated into the household. He claims that 80 percent of the occupancy of the home is in the kitchen and living area. He says, "People dine much more informally now as opposed to a decade ago. Formal dining and living spaces have become almost like museums."

DeWitt Talmadge Beall:
Colorful tile serves as an accent
to the wood cabinetry, brick and
other natural materials used
throughout this country kitchen.

▲

AUBERGINE MOUSSE WITH BEURRE BLANC
2 tablespoons olive oil
1 large eggplant, pared and diced
1/3 cup chopped shallots
3 garlic cloves, crushed
2 tablespoons tarragon, finely chopped
4 eggs
2 cups light cream
sea salt and freshly ground black pepper

For the sauce:
6 tablespoons unsalted butter
3 tablespoons white wine vinegar
5 tablespoons dry white wine
1 teaspoon chopped shallots
1 tablespoon heavy cream
sea salt and freshly ground black pepper

Heat the olive oil in a saucepan and gently sauté the diced aubergine (eggplant), shallots, garlic and tarragon. When the aubergine is soft, remove from the heat and leave to cool.

Place the contents of the pan into a blender container with eggs and purée. Add the cream, salt and pepper to blend again.

Preheat oven to 450 degrees. Butter 6-8 ramekins with some of the butter and divide the mixture evenly among the ramekins. Bake for 15-20 minutes.

While the mousse is baking, make the sauce. Put the vinegar, wine and shallots into a saucepan and reduce until there are about 2 tablespoons of liquid. Add the cream. When it begins to boil, lower the heat instantly and whisk in the butter.

To serve, pour some of the sauce into each ramekin to cover the top of the mousse.

HERITAGE CUSTOM KITCHENS
Ellen Cheever

Dubbed "Mother Kitchen" by her friends and colleagues, Ellen Cheever of Heritage Custom Kitchens discovered her recipe for stuffed portabello mushrooms while commuting to work in Pennsylvania.

"Every day I passed through Avondale, the mushroom capital of the United States," she says. "I discovered this recipe in a local magazine." Cheever recommends serving the mushrooms as a salad with sliced fresh tomatoes in the summer, or as an appetizer in the winter.

Cheever's business partner, Len Casey, agrees with her philosophy that "delicious food is also healthy food." He provided the recipe for smoked salmon. Once, in the village of Eze near Monte Carlo, Casey was served an appetizer of salmon with diced onions, tomatoes and capers, rather than the traditional approach of cream cheese and bread. When he returned to the United

States, Casey added the fresh endive leaves to create a healthy, easy and elegant appetizer.

Both recipes include fresh ingredients and can be prepared at the last minute. "The group approach to cooking is great!" says Cheever. "With today's lifestyle, the guests arrive, you hand them a glass of wine, someone starts washing the endive, and someone else starts dicing the onions. You visit as you prepare."

Describing her personal style as "casual elegance," Cheever believes the way food is served is as important as the food itself. "I love fresh flowers, a tablecloth and cloth napkins even for a Saturday afternoon picnic," she says.

DeWitt Talmadge Beall:
A long, crescent-shaped island divides kitchen and eating areas, while practically doubling the cook's working space.
▼

PORTABELLOS STUFFED WITH SPINACH AND SUN-DRIED TOMATOES
serves 6-8
6 portabello mushrooms, washed and stems removed
1 cup vinaigrette salad dressing
1 tablespoon olive oil
6 garlic cloves, crushed
1 onion, finely chopped
1 pound spinach, washed and dried
12 sun-dried tomatoes in oil, chopped
olive oil
juice of one lemon
salt, to taste
pepper, to taste
1/2 cup freshly grated Parmesan cheese

Marinate mushrooms in vinaigrette for 4-6 hours. Grill 6-8 minutes each side or broil about 6 inches from broiler 2-3 minutes each side. Cool.

Add oil to large fry pan and sauté garlic and onions until just tender. Add spinach and sun-dried tomatoes. Sauté until spinach wilts, 3-4 minutes. Add lemon, salt and pepper.

Place portabellos on baking sheet, sprinkle with Parmesan cheese. Mound spinach mixture onto each mushroom, dividing mixture evenly. Put mushrooms under broiler for 5 minutes or until hot and sizzling. Remove, cut into quarters and serve hot as an appetizer or side vegetable.

SMOKED SALMON APPETIZER
smoked salmon (estimate 2 ounces per person)
2 tomatoes
2 mild onions
endive leaves
capers

Dice smoked salmon, tomatoes and onions. Arrange on a platter with the endive leaves; endive leaves are used in place of bread squares. Add capers if you prefer.

COOK'S CUSTOM CABINETRY
Margaret Cook

"As a team, we share design concepts, which results in better service for our clients," says Margaret Cook. "One person may have an idea that another couldn't come up with."

At Cook's Custom Cabinetry, much of the team is composed of members of the Cook family. Margaret, her husband Ron, and her daughters Shelly and Melissa have all worked together to build the company.

Since the Cooks' Bolognese meat sauce is an old family recipe, it seems a perfect representation of their business. Margaret Cook often prepares the dish for family and friends.

The recipe came from her father, whose family originated in Bologna, Italy. Cook remembers her Irish mother preparing the dish when she was young. "My mother was a real home cook," she says. "I picked up a lot of my habits from her."

Cook's Custom Cabinetry: Colorful, mouth-watering presentation is achieved with ease when Spaghetti Bolognese is on the menu.

▶

Cook prepares her own pasta, so in the new kitchen she and her husband are designing, she has included a large baking area. "I like a baking area that is functional," she comments. "But each person's concept of cooking and prepping is different. We need to be sure that the kitchen is functional for every client."

CAVICCHI'S NORTHERN ITALIAN BOLOGNESE MEAT SAUCE
This recipe has been in our family for many years, and of course it may have varied through time. We hope you enjoy it as much as we do.

1/8 cup olive oil
1 medium onion, finely chopped
6 garlic cloves, minced
1 pound ground beef
1 pound ground pork
1 large can tomato paste
2 cans Italian peeled tomatoes (28 oz. each)
Note: crush/purée the tomatoes before adding
1 large carrot, cut into pieces
10 bay leaves
1 Knorr beef bouillon cube
2 pinches nutmeg
1/3 cup red wine

Heat olive oil; when hot, add garlic and onion; sauté. Add meat and let simmer until cooked. Add tomato paste and mix in. Add crushed tomatoes, water, carrot, bay leaves, nutmeg and wine; let simmer until mixture bubbles slowly, then add bouillon and crush as you add to the pot.
   The secret is to let the sauce simmer but not cook too fast. In approximately 3-1/2 hours, it will be done.
   Note: This is a thick sauce, so if it is thick in three hours, then it is ready. Cook your pasta and enjoy.

COOPER-PACIFIC KITCHENS
Kevin Cooper

With Neil Cooper, his wife Shirley, and sons Kevin, David and Steven all involved in running the company, Cooper-Pacific Kitchens seems to define "family business" on the West Coast. Beginning in the Midwest as a new home builder, Neil Cooper has been designing kitchens for 30 years.
   Kevin Cooper chose to share one of his grandmother's recipes that has been in the family for three generations. "We associate this dish with grandma and family get-togethers. We usually don't cook it ourselves because we have always thought my grandmother was the only person who could do it justice."

At home, Cooper and his wife often entertain informally. The couple's kitchen is designed to match their casual lifestyle. Says Cooper, "In my house, I want people to feel free to help themselves and drink a soda in the living room. Our kitchen is very user-friendly."

According to Cooper, "We sell dreams. We try to make kitchens fun and functional." Cooper claims that the reigning philosophy of Cooper-Pacific is "communication."

NAN'S NOODLES (As Told To Her Grandsons)
Many of our happy family memories revolve around Nan's kitchen. She was funny, generous, loving, and always had a smile for you. She also was a great cook! "Nan's Noodles" was always one of our favorites. Although she never used cookbooks or recipe cards, everything always tasted wonderful.
To be served with a roast

4 - 5 eggs
4 - 6 cups of white flour
salt and pepper as desired

Mix salt and flour. Pour eggs over flour and mix.
(It will be very dry - add a small amount of water if needed.) Dust breadboard and rolling pin with flour to prevent sticking. Roll mixture with rolling pin into very thin sheets. Cut sheets into strips, approximately 1 1/2" long. Stack strips and cut crossways approximately 1/4" wide.

Cook roast as desired with small amount of water in a covered roasting pan. Remove the roast and add water to the juices in the roasting pan. Heat juices to a simmer - do not boil. Add noodles slowly and stir continuously. Season to taste. Cook and stir until noodles are tender. Then serve with the roast beef.

bulthaup (LA) Inc: Full pull-out drawers make every inch of space available. Movable dowels create custom storage that keeps everything in place.

▼

DALIA KITCHEN DESIGN
Dalia Tamari

Dalia Tamari's recipe for Bavarian creme is a popular dessert in her native Israel. "We serve this dish when we entertain, which is often," she comments. Tamari has lived in the United States ten years, but most of her family is still in Israel. She travels at least once a year to visit them.

Tamari's own kitchens mirror two significant trends in design today. Her "weekday kitchen" in the city is very compact, efficient and European. Her country kitchen at her family's weekend home in New Hampshire is spacious, with room for her three children and guests to participate in food preparation. "If I stayed in the city on the weekends, I would probably keep working," she remarks.

Tamari strongly believes that "a kitchen should be a place that is efficient." Considering lighting, "friendly" floors, levels of working and cooking areas and materials of countertops, she strives to create a functional space for her clients.

Comments Tamari, "If I have a client who is working with a modest budget, I encourage him or her to invest in quality appliances rather than fancy cabinetry. We have to be practical about the use of kitchens."

BAVARIAN CREME
5 jumbo eggs
1 cup sugar
1 package lady fingers (plain)
1/2 cup amaretto
1/2 cup milk
1/2 teaspoon cream of tartar
100 grams walnuts (about 3.5 ounces)
1/2 pint cold whipping cream
2 packages unflavored gelatin
1/2 teaspoon lemon juice
1 bottle Hershey's chocolate syrup

Prepare 3 bowls for whipping:

Bowl 1: Place a large stainless steel bowl in the freezer with the beater attachment.

Bowl 2: While whipping the egg whites of all 5 eggs in a bowl, gradually add 1/3 cup of the sugar and 1/2 teaspoon of cream of tartar. Continue to whip until mixture obtains the consistency of stiff foam.

Bowl 3: Whip all 5 egg yolks and 1/3 cup of the sugar for a few minutes until the mixture obtains a pasty consistency and a margarine-like color.

In a small bowl, melt both gelatin packages in 1/2 cup boiling water until gelatin completely dissolves. After gelatin has melted, add the 1/2 cup milk and let the mixture stand for a few minutes.

Bowl 1: Take bowl out of the freezer and whip in it the whipping cream. Gradually add (while whipping continues) the last 1/3 cup sugar and the lemon juice. Continue whipping until foam is stiff. Do not overdo this whipping or the mixture might become buttery.

Arrange individual tops and bottoms of lady fingers on the bottom of a rectangular pan. Place them flat side down to create as complete a layer as possible. Sprinkle amaretto on top of the fingers layer.

Combine the mixtures in the small bowl and in bowl 3. Since the mixture in the small bowl is liquidy and we do not want to crush the foam in bowl 3 when we combine them, it is necessary to make the mixture in the small bowl less liquidy first. To do this, add a few tablespoons of the foam in bowl 3 to the small bowl until the mixture in the small bowl is a little foamy also. Then take the small bowl mixture and add it gradually to bowl 3, mixing in a folding motion.

Add bowl 1 to bowl 3, then add bowl 2 to bowl 3 also. Mix these all very carefully, again, so the mixture remains foamy. Pour entire mixture into the pan on top of the lady fingers. Chill in refrigerator for half a day.

Serve cold with a few lines of Hershey's syrup on top.

DE GIULIO KITCHEN DESIGN, INC.
Michael De Giulio

Michael De Giulio's recipe for peanut butter chocolate balls represents his family's affinity for chocolate. He laughs, "My wife has to hide anything chocolate from my children and me."

With four children aged six to seventeen, De Giulio says, "The kitchen is the hub of our home." The family especially enjoys preparing new chocolate treats and pizza together. "We use our kitchen as a gathering and living space," he says.

De Giulio sees each client's situation as unique. "At de Giulio kitchen design, we strive to reflect the personality of the client." De Giulio most enjoys building a relationship with clients, which enables him to move beyond just the practical elements of the space. "In essence, we are forming a personality," he remarks.

bulthaup (LA) Inc:
An ingenious arrangement centered around a sliding work surface helps integrate preparation, cooking and cleanup.

▼

Believing that kitchen design is the most challenging field of interiors because of its unique blend of technology, function and imagination, De Giulio has been involved in the business 24 years. "There are no boundaries to what we can do in the kitchen," he says. "We are limited only by our creativity."

PEANUT BUTTER CHOCOLATE BALLS
yields 75 to 80

1/4 pound butter, melted
2 cups confectioners' sugar
2 cups creamy peanut butter
2 cups crushed Rice Krispies
1/2 cup finely chopped pecans or peanuts
1 pound semi-sweet chocolate chips or dipping chocolate

In large bowl, combine all ingredients except chocolate. Stir and knead until well-blended. Chill at least 1 hour. Roll into 1-inch balls. Place on baking sheet and chill until firm, about 1 hour.

Melt chocolate in top of double boiler. Water should not touch bottom of pan. Using candy dipper or wooden skewer, dip each ball into melted chocolate. Place on wax paper. Chill until firm. Store in airtight container in refrigerator.

Ellen Cheever, Heritage Custom Kitchens: Highly detailed decorative moldings and arches recreate classical architectural elements.

▲

KITCHEN & BATH DESIGNS UNLIMITED, INC.
Thomas F. Leckstrom, CKD, President

A hunting, fishing, clamming and kayaking enthusiast, Thomas Leckstrom feels lucky to live in the beautiful environment of Cape Cod. He enjoys preparing his venison stew for family and friends on cold winter days.

Leckstrom designed his own kitchen, as well as those of his clients on the Cape, to incorporate the natural surroundings. "Around here, everyone has a view," he remarks. Leckstrom visits his clients' homes and asks them to complete questionnaires to help clarify their needs and tastes.

"It's very easy to draw up a kitchen when you know what the client wants," he says, adding that the most enjoyable part of his work is getting to know people and solving their design problems. In addition to his work on the Cape, Leckstrom has installed kitchens all along the East Coast.

In his own kitchen, Leckstrom created a peninsular eating area for his family. "We try to eat together as much as possible. I believe that is important," he says. He and his wife reserve their dining room for special occasions and entertaining.

Leckstrom has worked in the kitchen design business 25 years. He opened his Kitchen and Bath Designs Unlimited nine years ago, and his wife is now the "brains of the operation" as his office manager.

After designing more than two thousand kitchens, Leckstrom says he still feels like "each kitchen is my baby. I watch each stage of growth until it is done. Every client is special to us."

CAPE COD VENISON STEW OVER NOODLES
A wonderful meal for a cold winter's day on Cape Cod. Serve with a robust red wine like Louis Jardot Beaujolais.

1 venison steak, cubed
1 onion, chopped
2 cups beef broth
flour for dusting
salt and freshly ground pepper
olive oil
1/4 teaspoon cumin
egg noodles
1/4 cup flour
2 garlic cloves, minced
1/4 cup and 2 tablespoons butter
1/4 cup good brandy

Cube the venison. Season the flour with salt and pepper. Lightly toss the venison with the flour. Heat pan and add olive oil and 2 tablespoons butter. Sauté venison, onion and garlic. Stir frequently to prevent sticking. Sprinkle 1/4 cup flour over the meat and mix well. It will be very thick. Add brandy and cumin, stirring until the brandy reduces by one-half. After the brandy reduces, add 2 cups beef broth. Season with salt and pepper to finish. Stir in 2 tablespoons butter. Serve over buttered egg noodles. Enjoy!

Ellen Cheever, Heritage Custom Kitchens: Warm, natural colors provide a soothing backdrop for food preparation and socializing. Recessed ring pulls enhance the clean lines of the cabinetry.

▲

THE FREY COMPANY
Ron Frey

"The individualization of home interiors is one of the driving forces behind the increase in design products available today," remarks Ron Frey of The Frey Company. Frey explains that the myriad of woods, finishes, hardware, moldings and countertop materials available today make creating a personalized space easy.

However, choosing which materials will work best for the individual can often be challenging. To make the most functional decisions, comments Frey, "We get very close to the client. We try to ask the right questions and even gather nonverbal information."

"Designers have to remember that the client is the client," Frey says. "We do not intend for the room to look like the designer. We always bring something into the project, but we integrate our creativity with the client's needs."

Frey and his wife have just moved into a 70-year-old English tudor home with their three-year-old daughter. The couple plans to entertain often in their new space, making full use of its European style kitchen.

HONEY MUSTARD CHICKEN
serves 4
1 can (20 ounces) pineapple slices in juice
4 boneless skinless chicken breast halves
2 teaspoons vegetable oil
2 large garlic cloves, pressed
1 teaspoon thyme, crumbled
1 tablespoon cornstarch
1/4 cup each honey and Dijon mustard

Drain pineapple; reserve juice. Sprinkle chicken with salt and pepper to taste. Rub with garlic and thyme. Brown in hot oil in a non-stick skillet. Combine 2 tablespoons reserved juice with cornstarch. Combine honey and mustard; stir into skillet with remaining juice. Spoon sauce over chicken. Cover and simmer 15 minutes. Stir cornstarch mixture into pan juices. Add pineapple. Cook, stirring, until sauce boils and thickens.

HAGERMAN DESIGN GROUP, INC.
Dave Hagerman, CKD

Claiming that his wife Sherry is truly an "excellent cook," Dave Hagerman of Hagerman Design Group says, "I'm not a cook, but I love to get into the kitchen."

Hagerman turns meal preparation into an event for one of his family's favorite pesto dishes. "We would probably prepare this dish on a weekend," he says. "It's the kind of activity where everyone gets involved."

Even his two teenage sons help mix and press the pasta. "My sons have also been known to get into the kitchen and make cinnamon rolls on their own. They have actually prepared meals, too. They do their own part," says Hagerman.

The Hagermans cook together in the galley kitchen of the Cape Cod home they bought and remodeled five years ago. "When we are in the kitchen, we have this wonderful warmth surrounding us. It reflects our lifestyle and heritage."

During the warmer months, the Hagermans focus on their garden, using fresh cut herbs and flowers to enhance their meals.

"Fresh basil makes the pesto dish special," says Hagerman. "Both my wife and I love our garden. For some of our favorite dishes, or on special occasions like our anniversary, we will go out in our backyard among the flowers for this wonderful romantic meal."

The pasta and pesto recipes originate from different sources. The pesto is a blend of the recipes of a neighbor and a friend, and the pasta comes from Mrs. Hagerman's mother.

PESTO SAUCE
serves 4
2 cups lightly packed basil leaves - fresh
3 sprigs parsley - fresh
1/4 cup garlic cloves, crushed
1/4 cup olive oil
salt and pepper to taste

Put in food processor and blend until smooth.

Add:
1/8 cup pine nuts
Sprinkle into food processor a little at a time. Remove; put in bowl and add approximately 1/2 cup freshly grated Parmesan cheese.

EGG NOODLES
serves 4
2-4 eggs
1/2 cup milk
2 cups+ flour
salt to taste

Put 2 cups of flour and salt into mixer. Make an indention and put in 3 eggs. Mix slowly, adding milk. Continue mixing until the mixture cleans the sides of the bowl.

If needed, add the fourth egg and/or add more flour. Roll out and either cut or put through pasta machine for fettucine or spaghetti noodles.

JAMES R. IRVING
James R. Irving, ASID

James Irving's lifestyle requires frequent dining out with clients/friends, however, he reserves special evenings to cook for friends in his kitchen keeping room.

The room allows Irving to display his vast collection of antique platters and plates. It also features a prominent sitting area and antique French hooked rug, which cater to his preference for being surrounded by color and fabric.

"Today's larger kitchens often incorporate sitting areas," he says. "Tile, marble and granite are also quite popular. They're perfect for adding color and texture to the room."

Irving encourages homeowners to aim for originality in their kitchens.

"Be distinctive," he says. "The kitchen is the heart of the home. It should be inviting, but in a way that mirrors your personality."

KENTUCKY STYLE STUFFED PEPPERS
4 or 6 long green mango peppers
1 pound ground beef
1 cup onions, diced
1 cup rice, cooked
2 cups fresh tomato paste
celery or onion salt
pepper

Remove the tops and seeds from the peppers. Parboil for 15 minutes.
Stir ground beef in hot skillet for six minutes and add onions.
Mix meat, onions, and rice.
Place the peppers in a casserole dish and stuff with meat filling. Dilute the tomato paste with 1/4 cup of water. Pour the tomato paste over the stuffed peppers in the casserole dish. Sprinkle celery or onion salt and pepper over entire dish.
Bake at 300 degrees for 3 hours. Baste periodically.

JANE PAGE CREATIVE DESIGNS, INC.
Jane Page Crump

"Getting involved in kitchen design seemed natural to me," says Jane Page Crump of Jane Page Creative Designs. "In my work in residential design and space planning, I saw that the kitchen was the most popular room of the house." In addition, Crump has taught French cooking, and cooks extensively herself. "I recognize the importance of the kitchen," she adds.

A frequent entertainer, Crump comments, "Often I find myself too busy to cook the entire meal, but I can always find time for the preparation of the appetizers." One of her favorites is her "Elegant Avocados."

When Crump remodeled her own kitchen a few years ago, she changed from ladder-back chairs with a pine table to tub chairs and a round glass table. "Trends today are toward more comfortable seating," Crump explains. "Built-in television and entertainment centers, custom cabinets and softer lighting all lead to a kitchen that doesn't necessarily

de Giulio kitchen design, inc.: Elegant light fixtures, a marble table, and intricate crown moldings are just some of the elements that work together to create an unusual degree of sophistication in this spacious kitchen.

◀

look like a kitchen. We design kitchens to blend with the other rooms in the house."

Crump and her family cook often. Her two boys enjoy creating stir-fry. "However," Crump says, "when we get together to cook, I send my husband outside to grill. He's just too messy in the kitchen."

ELEGANT AVOCADOS
Ripened avocados*, cut in half
lemon juice
red caviar
sour cream
real bacon bits

Brush avocados with lemon juice. Have guests spoon red caviar, sour cream and bacon bits into the center. Another combination of condiments is sour cream, picante sauce and green chiles. Serve on small napkins held in the palm of the hand. A demitasse spoon can be used to eat the avocado and the stuffing. No cleanup, just throw away the shell! Everyone loves these.

*If only green avocados are available, purchase several days in advance and put in a paper bag in a closet to ripen.

KARLSON KITCHENS
David Karlson

The history of Karlson Kitchens reads like an American tale. In 1954, 19-year-old Ben Karlson arrived from Sweden in search of the American dream. Working his way up from unloading boxcars in a lumber yard to president of the lumber company, Karlson soon started his own business in 1965 — a home improvement center including kitchen and bath remodeling.

David Karlson began working for his father when he was 16 and, since Ben Karlson's death in 1991, David has run the company. "High style, strong design, strong function, strong service," is his description of a Karlson Kitchen.

Karlson believes that his job is to listen to his clients and determine their needs. "Sometimes they're not sure of their own priorities," Karlson explains. "We strive for a kitchen that looks good, works well and is accessorized properly," he adds.

Karlson offers the traditional recipes he associates with holidays and visits to Sweden, where most of

de Giulio kitchen design, inc.:
An innovative marbleized
treatment lends an air of mystery
to the range area. Rich under-
cabinet lighting intensifies the
effect.

his father's family still lives. "Even though I don't see them very often, I still feel close to my family in Sweden. I am very proud of my heritage."

SWEDISH APPLE CAKE WITH VANILLA SAUCE
6 servings
6 tablespoons butter
2-3/4 cups crushed zwieback crumbs (1 6-ounce package yields 2-3/4 cups of crumbs)
2 cups sweetened applesauce
vanilla sauce

Melt butter in pan. Add crumbs and stir until all crumbs are mixed with butter and lightly browned. Sprinkle 1/3 crumb mixture over bottom of shallow buttered 6-cup casserole or baking dish. Cover with 1 cup applesauce. Add another 1/3 of crumb mixture, cover with remaining 1 cup applesauce, and sprinkle top with remaining crumbs.

Bake uncovered in 350 degree oven 25-30 minutes. Chill apple cake in refrigerator. Unmold and serve with vanilla sauce.

VANILLA SAUCE
2 tablespoons sugar
1-1/2 teaspoons cornstarch
2 cups milk
3 egg yolks
1 teaspoon vanilla

Mix together sugar and cornstarch. Stir in milk. Cook, stirring constantly until sauce thickens. Reduce heat to very low and cook 8 minutes, letting sauce bubble only occasionally. Add some of the hot sauce to egg yolks, mix well and stir into remaining hot sauce. Cook 2 minutes longer. Remove from heat and add vanilla. Serve apple cake with warm or cold sauce.

SWEDISH MEAT BALLS

yields 70-80 meat balls	1/4 pound ground pork
2 cups soft bread crumbs	1/2 teaspoon pepper
2/3 cup milk	1 teaspoon nutmeg
1/2 cup minced onion	1 teaspoon paprika
3 eggs, slightly beaten	3 tablespoons flour
2 teaspoons salt	1 cup water
1 cup dairy sour cream	2 tablespoons minced parsley
1 pound ground beef	1 tablespoon concentrated meat extract
1/4 pound ground veal	3 tablespoons butter

Mix beef, veal and pork together. Soak bread crumbs in milk until softened. Add onion to 1 tablespoon butter in small saucepan and cook 3 minutes.

Mix softened bread, cooked onion and meat. Add eggs, salt, pepper, nutmeg and paprika. Mix thoroughly until very smooth and light.

Shape meat into small balls, dusting the hands with flour while shaping the balls. Melt 3 tablespoons of butter in a large frying pan. Add meat balls and fry until golden brown all over.

Remove from pan and add meat extract and 3 tablespoons flour. Stir until well blended. Add water and a few grains of pepper. Cook, stirring constantly until thickened. Reduce heat to very low and cook 5 minutes. Stir in sour cream, 1 tablespoon at a time; stir until thoroughly blended after each addition. Return meat balls to gravy, cover pan and simmer 10 minutes. Sprinkle with minced parsley.

SWEDISH BROWN BEANS
8-12 servings
1 pound Swedish brown beans
7 cups water
3/4 cup firmly packed brown sugar
3/4 cup dark corn syrup
1 tablespoon cold water
1/3 cup vinegar
2 teaspoons salt
1/2 teaspoon nutmeg
2 teaspoons cornstarch

Wash and drain beans. Add 7 cups water. Cover and let stand overnight.
   In the morning, bring to a simmering point. Cover tightly and simmer 3 to 3-1/2 hours or until tender.
   Add sugar, syrup, vinegar, salt and nutmeg. Mix cornstarch with 1 tablespoon cold water and stir into beans. Simmer uncovered 15 minutes. Serve hot.

KITCHEN & BATH CONCEPTS
Sara and Jim Meloy

Sara and Jim Meloy's six-year-old daughter enjoys helping her father prepare food at the island of their spacious kitchen. "Caesar salad is their specialty," claims Sara.

   Since she likes cooking, Sara Meloy prepares a meal nearly every night for the family to eat together. The Meloys also entertain often, inviting friends and family over to enjoy the home they designed and built six years ago.

   Jim Meloy has been in the kitchen design business 21 years. He believes his job is to guide the client to achieve the best use of space by using the best resources available. "We try to create a unity between construction and form so that all elements of the space blend to form the design," says Jim.

   The couple chose to share their cookie recipe because of its timelessness, reflecting their philosophy of design. "We strive to create kitchens that last," comments Sara Meloy. "There may be superficial changes over time, but the basic design should remain functional for years."

THUMBPRINT COOKIES
2 cups flour
3/4 cup confectioners' sugar
1-1/2 cups chopped pecans (set aside 1/2 cup)
1 cup softened butter
1 teaspoon vanilla

Mix flour, sugar, 1 cup nuts, butter and vanilla. Roll into 1-inch balls and roll in remaining nuts. Place on greased baking sheet and push down with thumb. Bake at 325 degrees for 15-18 minutes.

ICING
1 tablespoon softened butter
1 teaspoon vanilla
1 teaspoon milk (more if needed)
a few drops of food coloring
confectioners' sugar (1 box; more may be needed if more food coloring is used)
    Mix together and place in thumbprint of cookie when cool.

Karlson Kitchens: Cleverly designed waste-separation units take some of the drudgery out of cleanup and waste removal.
▲

KITCHEN CLASSICS, INC.
Nancy Hillner

Nancy Hillner and her husband, Ed, have run Kitchen Classics for 20 years. Before starting her career, Hillner enjoyed hosting dinner parties and preparing challenging, unusual menus.

She often used poultry for the main course so as not to offend the various palates, diets and cultures that crossed her threshold.

Nowadays, Hillner looks forward to brief mealtime respites from the demands of owning a business. With time at a premium, her menus have simplified but still revolve around poultry, vegetables and a green salad.

The Hillner family's evening meal is usually prepared between mid-afternoon appointments in one of the operational displays in the Kitchen Classics showroom. An Aga cooker gives Hillner the flexibility to hold a meal indefinitely.

Nancy and Ed believe a sit-down family meal preserves an important part of our past in today's hectic society.

"Machines such as the fax and computer have made life faster paced," Hillner says. "When people come home at the end of the day, they need peace. The kitchen should be a place of comfort."

SEVICHE
serves 6
2 pounds white solid fish fillet (sole or flounder)
1/2 pound small bay scallops
3 limes
3 lemons
2 red onions, sliced
2 green peppers, cut into 1-inch thin strips
2 teaspoons salt
1/4 teaspoon pepper
1/4 teaspoon cayenne pepper

Cut 2 pounds white solid fish fillet into 1-1/2 by 1/2 -inch strips. Combine in a large glass bowl with 1/2 pound small bay scallops, the juice of 3 limes, the juice of 3 lemons, 2 red onions, thinly sliced and cut into 1-inch pieces, and 2 green peppers, cut into 1-inch thin strips. Toss to combine mixture. Add 2 teaspoons salt, 1/4 teaspoon pepper, and 1/2 teaspoon cayenne pepper. Cover mixture and set in refrigerator overnight, or 2 to 3 days, if possible.

At serving time, spoon out individual servings using a slotted spoon.

CORNISH GAME HENS IN SALT CLAY
serves 6
Probably as old as cookery is the idea of baking birds in clay. Generations of chefs have used sculptor's clay. I use this version made from ordinary table salt and flour.

6 (12-ounce to one pound) Cornish game hens
1 tablespoon salt
1 teaspoon pepper
1/4 cup oil

Stuffing:
2 cups fresh white bread cubes 1/4-inch thick
1 cup diced, dried apricots
1 cup golden raisins
1 tablespoon basil
1-1/2 teaspoons powdered sage
1 teaspoon salt
1/4 teaspoon pepper
1/2 cup water
1/4 cup butter or margarine

1 batch clay:
(make each batch separately; you will need one per bird)
1-1/2 cups table salt
1 cup unsifted all-purpose flour
1/2 cup water

Prepare stuffing:
Combine in a large bowl: 2 cups fresh white bread cubes, 1 cup diced dried apricots, 1 cup golden raisins, 1 tablespoon basil, 1-1/2 teaspoons powdered sage, 1 teaspoon salt and 1/4 teaspoon pepper. Heat 1/2 cup water and 1/4 cup butter or margarine until melted. Pour into dry ingredients and toss well to combine.

Wash and pat dry 6 Cornish game hens. Use approximately 1/3 cup stuffing for each bird. Fold wings and tie legs together. Sprinkle each bird with a little of the 1 tablespoon salt and 1 teaspoon pepper. Brush each well with 1/4 cup oil. Wrap each completely in one layer of aluminum foil. Press foil tightly against body of bird to eliminate air pockets.

Make each batch of clay by combining 1-1/2 cups table salt, 1 cup unsifted flour and 1/2 cup water. Knead until smooth on a well-floured board. Roll out to a 9-inch square. Set foil-wrapped bird in center. Bring up clay around bird to seal completely. Repeat this process for each bird. Bake at 475 degrees for 1-1/2 hours. Cover with foil for last 30 minutes of cooking to prevent over-browning. Let cool 10 minutes. Set each in napkin-lined basket. Cover with another napkin. Have guests hit clay with a mallet to break it (keep it covered with a napkin to prevent splattering). Peel away clay and foil and lift bird from basket onto dinner plate.

Note: Because the salt clay sets so quickly, it is best to make only enough to cover one bird at a time. They can be done ahead of time and refrigerated until cooking time... if they are to be cooked that same day.

SNOW PEAS WITH WATER CHESTNUTS
serves 6
4 7-ounce packages frozen snow peas
1 teaspoon salt
1/4 teaspoon pepper
1 cup water chestnuts, drained and sliced
2 tablespoons butter or margarine, softened

Place 4 packages snow peas in a saucepan. Add 1 cup cold water that has been combined with 1 teaspoon salt and 1/2 teaspoon pepper. Place on heat and bring to a boil.

Cook 2 to 3 minutes longer. Drain well. To serve: Add 1 cup sliced and drained water chestnuts to snow peas. Toss with 2 tablespoons softened butter or margarine. Reheat briefly.

BLACK FOREST CHERRY CAKE
serves 8
1 (1 pound, 1-1/2 ounce) package double Dutch chocolate batter cake mix
2 eggs
1-1/2 cups water
1/4 cup kirsch wasser

filling:
2 (1 pound, 5 ounce) cans cherry pie filling
1/2 cup sugar

frosting:
3 (1/2-pint) cartons heavy cream
1/2 cup super fine sugar

Make up one package double Dutch chocolate batter cake mix according to label directions, using 2 eggs and 1-1/2 cups water. Divide evenly between two 8-inch cake pans that have been well greased and floured. Bake at 350 degrees for 35-40 minutes or until center springs back when lightly touched. Cool 10 minutes. Remove from pans. Cool completely. Cut each layer in half cross-wise. Sprinkle each of the four layers with 1 tablespoon kirsch wasser.

Prepare filling:
Drain both cans of cherry pie filling, using a slotted spoon (refrigerate syrup to be used on ice cream). Mix drained cherries with 1/4 cup sugar.

Prepare frosting:
Beat 3 cartons heavy cream until very stiff. Fold in 1/4 cup super fine sugar.

To assemble:
Place one cake layer on serving platter. Spread with 1/2 to 3/4 cup cherry filling and 3/4 cup whipped cream. Repeat this process with second and third layers. Place last layer on top and spread with remaining whipped cream. Chill at least 30 minutes.

Karlson Kitchens: Cooking utensils hang from a thin steel rail beneath the cabinets in this classically simple design.

▲

KITCHEN CONCEPTS, INC.
Cameron M. Snyder, CKD
Mercedes B. Aza

A native of Spain, Mercedes B. Aza follows the European tradition of making eating and cooking a social event. "On New Year's Eve," notes her husband and business partner, Cameron M. Snyder, "we began serving appetizers at 7:00 p.m., and we didn't get to the main course until 1:00 a.m. All of our guests are now familiar with the Spanish word - Tapear -, which denotes the ritual of sampling and sharing several appetizers."

"All my cooking is influenced by the Mediterranean style, in which flavor and presentation are extremely important," Mercedes says. "The food is flavorful, but not too spicy. The dishes are presented as an explosion of color, too tempting to resist. My grandmother used to say that there was no such thing as a poor appetite - only color-blind cooks with no imaginations."

Though she has a law degree and an MBA in Marketing, Mercedes spends most of her time in the home remodeling industry. She and Cameron work long hours in the same office but rarely talk at length during the day. "We try to leave work behind when we go home," Cameron says. "We cook as a release and a hobby."

Cameron came into the kitchen and bath business as a cabinet maker. He started Kitchen Concepts in 1976 after realizing he wanted to be more involved in design. Founded as a kitchen specialist, the company soon evolved into a design firm for the total home environment. "A remodeling project is an educational process for the client," he says. "My tip to any person remodeling their home is to interview designers until you find one with whom you're compatible with. It's important to be comfortable with the designer and to develop a positive relationship."

MERCEDES' PAELLA
4 garlic cloves, peeled*
2 teaspoons finely chopped fresh parsley
1 large red pepper, cut into strips
2 large fresh tomatoes, peeled* and puréed
1 cup fresh green peas
1 whole chicken, cut
1 pound medium shrimp, unpeeled

2 pounds clean mussels
1/2 pound "Chirlas" (or 8 small clams)
1 small lobster, boiled
2 pounds white Spanish rice
1 teaspoon powdered food colorant
olive oil
a pinch of saffron
salt
water
a big "Paella Pan" (available through Caphalon)

Boil the mussels, clams and shrimp and set aside. Reserve 8 cups of broth for later.

Sauté 3 garlic cloves in olive oil in the paella pan. Remove them, crush them with the fourth reserved clove and combine with the parsley. Sauté the pepper and reserve.

Sauté the chicken until golden brown and add salt to taste. Add the tomato purée and sauté for 5 minutes. Add the shellfish broth and bring everything to a boil. Add rice, saffron, and powdered food colorant.

Taste the rice after 15 or 20 minutes for desired firmness and flavor. When ready, add the garlic/parsley mix. Artistically place the peppers, green peas and reserved seafood for decoration. For the final touch, add a boiled lobster in the center and serve while hot.

*Tips:
Peeling Garlic Cloves
To peel whole garlic cloves, trim off the ends and drop cloves into boiling water for 5 to 10 seconds. Immediately, plunge them into cold water and drain. The peels should slip right off. If the cloves are to be minced, trim off the ends and crush them with a flat side of a large knife. The peels can then be easily removed.

Peeling Tomatoes
Place tomatoes, one at a time, in a saucepan of simmering water for about 10 seconds (or 30 seconds if they are not fully ripened). Do not add more than one tomato to the hot water at a time or the temperature will drop rapidly and the tomatoes will stew before the skins can be removed. Immediately after, plunge them into a bowl of cold water for another 10 seconds. The skins will peel off easily with a knife. Purée the tomatoes with a food processor slowly to keep sauce texture.

KITCHEN DISTRIBUTORS
Tom Hartman

Founded 41 years ago, Kitchen Distributors has earned a reputation based on a knowledgeable, creative design team and strong attention to detail. "I personally go through every plan that comes through this office," says Tom Hartman, CKD. "We have a good system of checks and balances."

Hartman's father opened the business in 1953 as a wholesale distributor of cabinets. The company's focus eventually shifted toward customized cabinetry. When

Karlson Kitchens: Gently rounded horizontal oak edges create an atmosphere of harmonious softness – an excellent example of how a simple design can look exclusive.

▲

his father passed away in 1974, Tom, his sister and mother took over the business and sharpened the custom focus even more.

"Since we are a family business, our name and reputation are always at stake," says Hartman. "Staying in business so long has involved a lot of effort."

Today, the six-member design team cooperates to create kitchens that are functional and aesthetically pleasing works of art. "By interviewing clients and having them complete an extensive survey, we develop an overall theme or look that will work in the best way possible for each individual," Hartman says.

"The kitchen used to be four walls back in a corner of the house," he adds. "Now, as the nerve center of the home, it makes a definite statement about its owner."

KITCHENS BY DEANE INC.
Kelly Stewart

Kelly Stewart enjoys working "on the front line" with the team of seven designers at Kitchens by Deane. "We are constantly collaborating, even when we are staring at that blank sheet of paper," he remarks.

"We are a progressive team," Stewart asserts. "Today it is extremely important to stay abreast of changes in the field." Having trained new kitchen designers for ten years, and served as the CKD coordinator for southern New England, he finds it absolutely necessary to keep pace with industry trends.

"The more you give end-users, the more they will demand," Stewart remarks. "Today's client is very well-educated."

As consumers demand a more authentic traditional look, Stewart sees a return to "custom finishes, hardware and moldings that truly look two hundred years old." Says Stewart, "Kitchen design is much more intensely detailed than ever before. Nothing is generic."

The traditional kitchen of Stewart's country farmhouse features a collection of antique plates. Stewart and his wife and two daughters enjoy cooking together, although Stewart jokes, "I am a survival cook. No one starves when I am preparing the food."

Kitchens by Stephanie, Ltd.
Stephanie J. Witt, CKD, CBD

"Cooking is no longer something we do for survival," says Stephanie Witt. "In most families, both spouses work outside the home. This trend has transformed kitchens from hidden workrooms into open areas integrated into our living space. The kitchen has become the center for social and family gatherings."

At the center of most Witt family gatherings is their special rhubarb pie. The recipe, a springtime favorite, has been passed down through four generations.

"We associate rhubarb pie with a family gathering, like birthdays and reunions — a time when people get together," Stephanie says. "The biggest problem with making a good rhubarb pie is finding fresh rhubarb," adds daughter Kyle. "Most grocery stores carry it in the spring, but a friend with a bountiful rhubarb patch is probably the best source."

When working with a family to remodel their kitchen, Stephanie's first step is to learn how that family lives. "The best way I know to design a kitchen that will work for a family, is to get to know them by making friends," she says.

But her design work often spreads well beyond the kitchen. "I frequently design living rooms and dining rooms around the kitchen," Stephanie says. "It's similar to the way our family plans a spring picnic - around the rhubarb pie."

STEPHANIE'S MOM'S RHUBARB PIE
yields 1 pie
The secret of this recipe is to mound the rhubarb high in the shell because it shrinks when you bake the pie. If the rhubarb is juicy, add more flour for a custardy texture; if it is tart, add sugar.

1 pie crust
rhubarb
1-1/2 - 2 cups sugar
1 lemon
1 egg
3 tablespoons+ flour
butter

Make a crust; dice rhubarb. Squeeze 1 lemon; add juice to 1 beaten egg. Add 1-1/2 to 2 cups sugar (depending on the tartness of the rhubarb) and 3 tablespoons flour. Blend and pour over fruit, then dot with butter. Enough for 1 pie. Bake at 450 degrees for 15 minutes. Then decrease heat to 350 degrees and continue baking for 45 more minutes.

de Giulio kitchen design, inc.: A herringbone wood floor provides a warm contrast to the bright colors that are otherwise predominant. Note how the colorful surrealistic painting draws the eye.

▲

KITCHENSMITH
Shirley McFarlane

Shirley McFarlane chose to share her shrimp mold recipe because it came from one of her first clients 15 years ago. "The client had a party for everyone involved in remodeling her kitchen," says McFarlane. "She gave me the recipe, and I still use it all the time."

McFarlane and her husband enjoy the fair climate of Atlanta, often entertaining and grilling outside. "All of our rooms open in some way out onto the pool and patio area," she comments. "We take full advantage of the nine months of warm weather here."

"I grew up in the kitchen design industry," McFarlane explains, adding that her father ran a kitchen design business in Denver. "He used to bring home miniature cabinet samples and set them up for my sisters and me."

When McFarlane moved to Atlanta with her husband and began designing for Kitchensmith, she discovered that president Herb Schmidt had worked for her father. "Herb and I work well together," she remarks, "partly because we are committed to delivering outstanding design, service, and products."

When designing kitchens, McFarlane completes a survey to determine how to best create a functional space. She sees most of her clients using kitchens on the weekends. She says, "I don't know many families that can eat dinner together every night at six o'clock. They are simply too busy."

SHRIMP MOLD
serves 20
3 cups shrimp
1/2 cup celery, chopped
1 grated onion
2 envelopes unflavored gelatin
1 tablespoon Worcestershire sauce
tabasco to taste
1/3 cup cold water
1 can tomato soup (heated)
12 ounces softened cream cheese
2 cups mayonnaise
1 teaspoon salt

Make several hours ahead, even a day, so that it will be firm.
Beat softened cream cheese until fluffy. Dissolve gelatin in water and add to heated soup. Combine with cream cheese and beat with electric mixer until smooth. Fold in other ingredients and pack in lightly oiled mold; chill.
Unmold and serve with crackers.

Kitchens Unique by Lois
Lois Kirk

"I'm just a plain country girl," says Lois Kirk. "I serve lamb like it was served years ago. This dish is something I always anticipated at my grandmother's. Now my five grandchildren come to my house for lamb on Easter and the holidays."

Since Kirk often works 14 hours a day, she and her husband find little time to cook during the week. "We cook on the weekends and holidays," she says. "And in the summertime, we barbecue with friends."

But Kirk believes that kitchens aren't just for cooking, especially today. "We are going back to the frontier years, when the kitchen and the living room were one room," she says. "Now you often find a loveseat or a narrow-backed chair in the kitchen for people to relax and talk."

Kirk believes that the kitchen makes a home. She often lets the aroma of her cooking linger in the house rather than turn on a fan. "The odors of cooking are good for the home, whether it is a lamb roasting, coffee brewing or bread baking," she says. "I don't believe that it all has to be blown out."

Kirk also points out that families today usually gather in the kitchen when it's time to make big decisions. "The kitchen has rich associations for most people," she says. "It's where the family congregates to discuss the day's problems and events. Somehow, we always come back to the kitchen."

Karlson Kitchens: In today's sophisticated kitchens, precisely crafted interior fittings often lie behind the beautiful scenes created by dramatic exteriors.

LEG OF LAMB AS PASSED THROUGH THE YEARS
serves 10

1 package lamb (about 5 pounds)	1 tablespoon Worcestershire sauce
vegetable oil	1/4 cup lemon juice
salt	1 teaspoon dry mustard
1/2 teaspoon pepper	a bit of hot sauce
1/2 cup water	1/4 teaspoon paprika
1/2 cup red wine	1 garlic clove, pressed
2 tablespoons vinegar (wine)	1 medium onion, grated

Rub lamb with 1 tablespoon of oil and 1 tablespoon salt and pepper. Place on grill over low coals or in oven set at 325 degrees. Cook about 45 minutes to an hour, turning occasionally and brushing with oil.

Combine water, wine, vinegar, Worcestershire sauce, lemon juice, mustard, hot sauce, paprika, garlic, onion, 1 tablespoon oil and 1/2 teaspoon salt in a saucepan. Bring mixture to a boil, and brush lamb with sauce. Cook 1 hour longer to desired degree of doneness.

Turn on broiler after final brushing to glaze slightly.

LA ASSOCIATES
Linda Lieber

Karlson Kitchens: Slide-out drawers from Becker Zeyco can be pulled open all the way, making it easy to find and remove items inside.

▲

"I love to be experimental when I cook," says Linda Lieber. "I don't like to cook the same thing twice." Last year, in a quest for holiday recipes that "didn't use 14 pounds of butter," Lieber discovered her low-fat pumpkin cheesecake squares in a cooking class.

While Lieber cooks less often and less formally than she did years ago, she and her husband enjoy the wealth of options available today. "Now we can choose red, green, yellow or purple peppers. We have hundreds of other types of produce, fresh herbs and wonderful bread available all the time," she says.

Lieber describes her kitchen as expandable. "I can comfortably prepare and serve a meal for two or twenty people," she explains. She designs her clients' kitchens with the same goal. "The kitchen might as well be wonderful since everyone gathers there anyway," she remarks. "We have moved way beyond the work triangle. Kitchens are more individualized today."

Lieber and her partner, Beryl Armstrong, founded LA Associates ten years ago. Although Lieber had experience in German cabinetry, she claims, "My main qualification was my extensive knowledge of what goes on in the kitchen. Not only did I cook every day, I also entertained often on an elaborate scale. And I loved it!"

PUMPKIN SPICE CHEESECAKE SQUARES
1 small can pumpkin (not pie filling)
1 teaspoon cinnamon
2 teaspoons chopped crystallized ginger
1/4 teaspoon each mace, nutmeg, cloves
1/2 cup gingersnap cookie crumbs
1 16-ounce Friendship whipped cottage cheese (1% fat)
2 8-ounce packages light cream cheese at room temperature
1 cup sugar
1 teaspoon vanilla
2 eggs or egg substitute equivalent

Preheat oven to 325 degrees. Spray 9-inch baking pan with Pam. In the food processor, whip pumpkin until smooth. Add all the cheeses and process 1 minute, stopping once to scrape mix down. Add sugar, spices, ginger, vanilla and eggs. Process 1 more minute, scraping once again. Pulse in gingersnaps. Scrape into prepared pan and bake for 1 hour and 15 minutes (can be baked in a water bath if desired).

Cool for 20 to 30 minutes in the oven with the door partially open, and then move to a rack to cool the rest of the time. Chill for at least 8 hours.
Calories: 250
Fat: 10 grams with eggs, 8 grams with egg substitute (90 or 72 fat calories)

LaMantia Kitchen Design Studio
Lynn Larsen
Joe LaMantia

According to Joe LaMantia and Lynn Larsen, "Sunday Pasta Sauce" improves as the day goes on. "I start this sauce on Sunday mornings in the fall and let it simmer throughout the day while we watch football," says LaMantia. "Sometimes we don't even get around to making the pasta, we just dip bread in the sauce." The sauce is a conglomeration of recipes from his mother and grandmother, along with his own additions.

With backgrounds in construction and architecture, respectively, LaMantia and Larsen turned to kitchen design because of its personal slant. Both enjoy working directly with clients to determine their needs and ideas.

"I like to get people excited about their kitchens from the very beginning," says Lynn Larsen. "I search for that something special that makes their eyes light up." Larsen looks for unique aspects of her clients' lives, hobbies or families to incorporate into the kitchen. "It may just be a collection of antique bowls or plates, but it must be personal," she comments.

LaMantia adds that altering height and depth to create visual excitement further individualizes a space. "But you need to create a focal point," he says.

When designing a kitchen, the pair take into consideration its relative immortality. "We are only in our clients' lives for six months or a year, but the kitchen is there as long as they are in the house," remarks Larsen. LaMantia adds, "That is why we must ensure the client's satisfaction."

SUNDAY PASTA SAUCE
4 garlic cloves
1 medium onion, peeled and chopped
4 tablespoons olive oil
10 Italian sausages
20 meatballs (recipe follows)
6 pork spareribs
1 pound boneless pork (no fat)
3-4 28-ounce cans tomato sauce
3-4 28-ounce cans crushed tomatoes
1 12-ounce can tomato paste
1 tablespoon sugar
10 large fresh basil leaves, coarsely chopped
2 tablespoons oregano
1/2 cup Parmesan and Romano cheese, grated

Karlson Kitchens: Tambour cupboards create storage space for small appliances while adding distinctive style.
▼

In a large stainless steel or enamel pot, gently fry garlic and onion in the oil until golden brown. Brown sausages in the same pan and set aside. Have browned meatballs ready. Brown ribs and pork and set aside. Pour off the fat and (in the same pan) add tomatoes and tomato paste. Gently heat to a boil, stirring often.

Add meats, sugar, basil, oregano and cheese to the hot sauce. Stir gently. Let simmer for 2 hours, stirring occasionally. Skim off as much fat as possible.

Serve on any type of your favorite pasta. Sprinkle with additional basil and cheese.

MEATBALLS

2 pounds ground chuck	1 tablespoon olive oil
2 cups Italian flavored bread crumbs	2 garlic cloves, chopped very fine
2 eggs	1 onion, chopped fine
1/3 cup milk	2 teaspoons oregano
1 cup fresh parsley, chopped	2 teaspoons basil
1/2 cup grated cheese	

Place all ingredients in a large bowl and mix thoroughly. Shape into medium-sized meatballs. Place on foil on a cookie sheet and bake until brown at 350 degrees (approximately 1/2 hour). Gently place in your own hot pasta sauce and cook at least 1 hour.

MADISON DESIGN GROUP
Gary Fried

"The kitchen is no longer an isolated room with a singular purpose," says Gary Fried of Madison Design Group. "Kitchens today are gathering and entertaining areas." Fried believes a major factor in the shifting roles of kitchens is changing lifestyles.

"There is no traditional family dinner at 5:00 p.m. or 6:00 p.m. each day," comments Fried. "In many cases, both parents work, or there may be a single parent working with an older relative sharing the home. Kitchens reflect the composition of the household."

Fried adds that more homes today include multiple cooks. "Many times both members of a couple cook, or there may be a parent or relative around who likes to prepare food." In these cases, Fried explains, "A convenient space and functional accessories make it not only easy, but desirable to work in the area."

To integrate the kitchen into the rest of the home, Fried sees more cabinetry that is consistent with the furnishings in adjoining rooms. "We are seeing cabinets in the kitchen as opposed to kitchen cabinets," he remarks. "As kitchen designers, it is increasingly important that we work with the interior designer to ensure that there is a consistency between the different areas of the house. That is one of our primary objectives."

NDM KITCHENS, INC.
Nancy Mullan

Nancy Mullan of NDM Kitchens acquired her recipe for classic French vinaigrette "many, many years ago" in Paris. "I was young and I had people over for dinner, but I didn't know how to cook," says Nancy. One of her guests, Prince Roland de Broglue, prepared the salad dressing and taught her how to make it.

Mullan swears by the peanut butter jar to measure, mix and store the dressing, which she uses on everything - salads, vegetables, and leftovers. "I chose this recipe because it is what I use the most throughout the year," she says.

"My philosophy of kitchen design comes directly from the fact that I don't really like to cook," Nancy explains. "I want everything to function perfectly and to be right where I need it, when I need it. I want my kitchen to

Kitchen Classics, Inc.: Spring seems to be all around in this spacious kitchen designed around a pastel color scheme. The overscaled range hood also serves as an intriguing architectural element.

▼

look terrific so that everyone wants to be in the kitchen with me and I don't feel left out."

Mullan asserts that even when you plan to have people in the living or dining room, everyone gathers in the kitchen. Mullan says, "Even in showhouses, at the end of the day, people end up in the kitchen because that is where they feel most comfortable."

PRINCE ROLAND'S SALAD DRESSING
a.k.a. NANCY MULLAN'S SALAD DRESSING
(really just basic French vinaigrette)

The only measurement to remember here is 1 part wine vinegar to each 3 parts of good extra-virgin olive oil.

You can mix enough for a salad for four by putting a tablespoon of vinegar and three tablespoons of oil in a bowl, adding mustard, salt and pepper to taste, and beating well with a whisk or a fork.

The best way to make it is in a peanut butter jar that has measurements marked on the side. Put into the jar:

1/4 cup wine vinegar
3/4 cup extra-virgin olive oil
4 dollops of Dijon mustard*
4 pinches kosher salt
20 turns of the pepper mill

Put the top on the jar and shake well. Whatever you don't use can be stored indefinitely in the refrigerator. Salt does lose some flavor when refrigerated, though, so check when you use again in case it needs more.

*A dollop is as much as you can scoop out of the mustard jar on a broad-bladed table knife.

nuHaus
Doug Durbin

Doug Durbin heads the design team at nuHaus and has four children. He says, "Despite appearances, my lifestyle is not as hectic as you may think. I have made certain choices, and I am happy with them. I enjoy working and spending time at home with my family."

When the Durbins remodeled their own kitchen, they took out most of the walls and all of the doors. Whether their children, aged four to eleven, are doing homework or watching television in the family room, there is a sense of togetherness. "Our house has a casual, homey feeling," says Durbin.

As he designs kitchens, Durbin aims to involve his client in each step of the process. "The client needs to be intimately tied to all of the decisions," he remarks.

"It is our job to help clients understand the impact of the issues we are facing."

"We work very hard at maintaining a team approach to design," he continues. "I oversee an incredibly talented staff, but as good as we like to think we are individually, we can always use a fresh set of eyes or new ideas."

Durbin adds that taking heed of the client ultimately leads to satisfying results. "It doesn't take a rocket scientist to sit down and listen to people."

DOUG'S SPRING LOBSTER WITH FRESH BABY VEGETABLES
serves 4

No dish says "springtime" like this brilliantly colored mixture of lobster and baby vegetables garnished with fresh herbs. This extravagant, elegant preparation is one of my favorites of Chef Robuchon's dishes, for it sings of freshness, delicacy, richness and vivacity. If you are able to obtain female lobsters, be sure to reserve the precious dark green coral. The coral can be mixed with butter and cream and quickly cooked at the last minute to create a bright red lobster sauce, one of Chef Robuchon's signatures. If baby vegetables are not available, trim standard size fresh vegetables down to size. You don't need to slavishly follow the suggested number and variety of vegetables, but for a colorful presentation, choose a combination of at least four. In this recipe, much of the preparation can be done in advance with a few moments of last minute cooking at serving time.

Wine suggestion: An intense wine, such as a Batard-Montrachet, from Burgundy

Equipment: 4 bamboo skewers
1 recipe ginger shellfish court bouillon (recipe follows)
4 live Maine lobsters (1 pound each), preferably female
1 to 4 tablespoons unsalted butter, softened (for the coral)

VEGETABLES
16 baby carrots, peeled, greens trimmed to 1 inch from base
3 tablespoons sugar
7 tablespoons unsalted butter
sea salt and freshly ground white pepper to taste
16 baby purple-top white turnips, scrubbed, greens trimmed to 1 inch from base
16 fresh baby onions (or substitute pearl onions)
7 ounces snow peas, ends trimmed, strings removed
8 ounces fresh chanterelle mushrooms, trimmed and brushed clean (or substitute domestic mushroom caps, trimmed, cleaned and quartered)
1 tablespoon freshly squeezed lemon juice (for domestic mushrooms)

Sauce:
7 tablespoons unsalted butter, chilled
sea salt and freshly ground white pepper to taste
1 tablespoon freshly squeezed lemon juice (optional)
1 tablespoon heavy cream
3 tablespoons minced fresh ginger
small bunch fresh chervil or flat-leaf parsley leaves, for garnish

1. Blanch the lobsters: In a large pot, bring the court bouillon to a rolling boil. Thoroughly rinse the lobsters under cold running water. With scissors remove the rubber bands restraining the claws, and plunge the lobsters, head first, into

the court bouillon. Counting from the time the lobster hits the water, cook for 2 minutes. With tongs, remove the lobsters from the court bouillon and drain. (Note that the lobster meat will not be fully cooked at this point.) Reserve 1-1/3 cups of the court bouillon for the sauce.

2. Remove the lobster meat: Twist each large claw off the body of the lobster. Gently crack the claw shells with a nutcracker or hammer, trying not to damage the meat. Extract the meat with a seafood fork. It should come out in a single piece. Set aside. To remove the meat from the tail, use scissors to cut lengthwise through the back of the lobster, and extract the tail meat in a single piece. With a small knife, remove the long, thin intestinal tract running the length of the tail meat.

Remove and discard the lumpy head sac, located near the eyes. Remove and reserve the soft green strip of tomalley (liver) from the upper portion of the body cavity. Remove and carefully reserve the dark green coral that runs parallel to the liver, if present. Pass the coral of each lobster through a fine-mesh sieve, and mix with 1 tablespoon butter for each coral. The lobster butter will be used later to prepare the sauce. Cover securely and refrigerate.

Gently roll the tail meat into a neat spiral, securing it with a bamboo skewer. Trim the skewers if necessary. Place all the lobster meat on a clean plate, cover securely, and refrigerate until just before serving time. The lobster can be prepared to this point up to 4 hours in advance.

If desired, carefully rinse the head and feathery antennae, and with scissors cut the shell in half lengthwise to use as a garnish. Cover securely and refrigerate.

3. Prepare the root vegetables: In a small saucepan with a tight fitting lid, combine the carrots, 1 tablespoon of the sugar, and 1 tablespoon of the butter over moderate heat. Season, cover and cook until tender, shaking the pan from time to time, 10 to 15 minutes. (Cooking time will vary according to the size and freshness of the vegetables.) Drain and set aside. Repeat with the turnips and onions, cooking each with 1 tablespoon sugar and 1 tablespoon butter.

4. Prepare the snow peas: Prepare a large bowl of ice water. Bring a large pot of water to a boil. Add 1 tablespoon salt per quart of water, and add the snow peas. Cook until tender, about 4 minutes. Remove with a slotted spoon and transfer to the ice water. Once cooled, drain and set aside.

5. Prepare the asparagus: Bring a small deep saucepan of water to a boil. Add the asparagus, standing up, and cook just until the lower portions are crisp tender, about 4 minutes. Add boiling water to cover the tips, and continue cooking for 2 to 3 minutes. Remove with tongs and place in the ice water. Drain and set aside, removing the twine.

6. Prepare the mushrooms: In a medium skillet, combine the mushrooms and the remaining 1 tablespoon of butter over moderate heat (if you are using domestic mushrooms, add the lemon juice along with the butter). Season, cover and cook until tender, about 5 minutes. Drain and set aside.

7. Finish cooking the lobster: In a large non-stick skillet, heat 4 tablespoons of the butter over moderately high heat. Generously season the lobster pieces with salt and pepper. Sauté the lobster gently for 3 to 4 minutes on each side, removing the faster cooking claw meat as soon as the meat firms and turns a bright sunset red. As the lobster cooks, spoon the butter over the meat to keep it moist. Remove the lobster from the pan, transfer to a large serving platter, and keep warm. In the same skillet, add the reserved 1-1/3 cups court bouillon to the butter over high heat; reduce for 2 to 3 minutes. Add the lemon juice, and whisk to blend. Add the cream to the coral butter mixture, and stir to blend. Add this to the sauce, whisking constantly. Do not let the sauce boil. The coral should turn the sauce a bright red. Add the minced ginger. Off the heat, swirl in 3 tablespoons chilled butter. Taste for seasoning.

8. In a large skillet, combine all the reserved vegetables with the remaining 3 tablespoons butter over moderate heat. Heat just to warm through, stirring gently, about 1 to 2 minutes. Taste for seasoning.

9. To serve: Remove the skewers from the lobster. Spoon the sauce over the lobster, and arrange the vegetables on top. If desired, place the reserved lobster shells decoratively around the edges of the platter. Sprinkle with the chervil or parsley leaves, and serve immediately.

GINGER SHELLFISH COURT BOUILLON
yields 4 quarts
Fragrant with ginger, fennel, anise and orange, this is a marvelously aromatic court bouillon, ideal for cooking all fresh shellfish. The court bouillon may be prepared several hours in advance, then brought to a rolling boil at cooking time. If you are cooking several particularly large shellfish, such as lobsters, you may need to double the recipe.

Equipment: 1 8-quart stockpot
1 large carrot, cut into thin rings
1 large onion, cut into thin rings
1 celery rib, thinly sliced
2 plump fresh garlic cloves
1 ounce peeled and trimmed fresh ginger
1 teaspoon fennel seeds
1 teaspoon white peppercorns
1 segment of star anise
3 tablespoons coarse sea salt
2 cups dry white wine, preferably a Chardonnay
2 teaspoons white vinegar
grated zest (orange rind) of 1 orange

Bouquet garni: Several parsley stems, celery leaves, and sprigs of thyme, wrapped in the green part of a leek and securely fastened with cotton twine.
    In a large stockpot, combine 4 quarts of water with carrot, onion, celery, garlic, ginger, bouquet garni, fennel seeds, peppercorns, anise and salt. Cover and bring to a boil over high heat. Reduce the heat and simmer gently for 20 minutes. Add the wine, vinegar and orange zest, and simmer for 5 minutes more. To cook shellfish, bring to a rolling boil before immersing the shellfish. (Strained, the court bouillon may be refrigerated for up to 2 days. Do not freeze, for it could become bitter.)

PAST BASKET
David and Linda McFadden

Linda McFadden and her husband David work together to run their business established 19 years ago just outside of Chicago. Linda sells decorative accessories while David runs a cabinetry showroom. Although they entertain often, the couple does not have much idle time. They like to prepare dishes such as the antipasto as guests arrive.

Linda, who is more concerned with the visual presentation of food than the number of days involved in its preparation, serves the antipasto at parties or to her clients at Past Basket. "This dish is full of flavor," she says, "and when it is on a pretty platter surrounded by fresh greens, it looks very attractive."

As for her cooking, Linda says she uses fresh vegetables for steaming and salads. "I am more interested in healthy foods that are quick to prepare than creamy gourmet meals," she explains, adding that her cooking style has evolved over the years as people have become more conscious about healthier living. "Our kitchen has changed as well," says Linda. "Now we need more refrigeration to store more fresh foods."

When the couple restructured their home they realized that they enjoyed living in the kitchen area, so they created a "mini-apartment" out of the kitchen. "Our kitchen is now purely for cooking and seating, and we have created a little eating area in the adjoining room," explains Linda.

David McFadden observes that their transition mirrors that of his clients. "Today, kitchens are more of a living space," he asserts. "People want an area for food preparation and informal dining along with a family room."

Rutt of New York City: A custom island in blanc maple helps create an atmosphere reminiscent of provincial France.
▲

ANTIPASTO

The most difficult thing about this fabulous recipe is finding some of the ingredients. It is easy to assemble and can be embellished for serving to a crowd of any degree of "food sophistication."

1 small can tuna in oil
1 can sardines in tomato sauce
1/2 cup olive oil
1 small can tomato paste
1 teaspoon oregano
1 small jar pimento stuffed olives

1 small jar tiny sweet gherkin pickles
1 small jar sweet cocktail onions
1 small jar pickled green beans
1 small jar pickled cauliflourettes
1 small can mushroom caps

Stir together tomato paste, olive oil and oregano. Add flaked tuna with all its oil. Remove tails and bones from sardines and add to mixture with all of its sauce. Add all other ingredients without the liquid, reserving some liquid from the pickled ingredients to add at the end if more moisture is needed. Refrigerate overnight, stirring a few times to mix all flavors.

Pile on a serving platter and garnish with fresh grape leaves, fresh purple and green basil and party rye bread slices.

Purdy's Design Studio
William Purdy

With a background in architecture, William Purdy believes that "form follows function." He explains, "Kitchens must function first. I add decorative ideas after I plan the functional aspects of the space."

At home, Purdy's two teenage sons are "into every sport and are always hungry" so he and his wife have become adept at preparing meals within minutes. The family barbecues dishes such as his London broil on weekends.

Purdy first became involved in kitchen design when he graduated from college with a degree in architecture and his parents asked him to help remodel their kitchen. Twenty-five years later, he has seen many changes in the field.

"I used to only interview with the woman about how the kitchen should be designed," he comments. "Now, the man may be the only member of the household specifying the kitchen." Purdy adds that cubbies for children and their homework, space for pets, sitting areas and desks or craft areas all reflect the centrality of the kitchen in homes today.

Kitchens By Deane, Inc.:
Vibrant red cabinetry creates a kitchen packed with drama, emotion – and confidence.
◄

Menu:
London Broil
Roasted Corn
Bananas Foster

LONDON BROIL STEAK BARBECUE
serves 6-8
First cut top round, two inches thick (3-4 pounds)
1/3 cup red wine
3 tablespoons salad oil
2 tablespoons honey
2 tablespoons chopped green onions with tops
1 garlic clove mashed
1/4 teaspoon dried oregano (or 1 teaspoon fresh oregano)
1/4 teaspoon dried basil (or 1 teaspoon fresh basil)
3/4 teaspoon salt
1/4 teaspoon paprika

Marinate meat 4 to 5 hours or overnight in the mixture of wine, salad oil, honey, chopped green onions, garlic, oregano, basil, salt and paprika.
    Drain and save marinade.
Grill over hot coals (about 10 to 12 minutes on each side for rare meat), basting with remaining marinade. I usually plug in a meat thermometer, if time allows to set up rotisserie.
    Slice thinly across the grain and serve on a heated platter.

ROAST CORN ON THE COB
Remove husks and silk from corn. Place each ear on a piece of aluminum foil. Spread liberally with butter or margarine. Wrap aluminum foil securely around each ear of corn. Don't seal seam but fold or twist around ends (that way corn will roast instead of steam).
    Place on grill and roast over hot coals 15 to 20 minutes until tender, turning frequently.

BANANAS FOSTER
serves 1
2 tablespoons brown sugar
1 tablespoon butter
1 ripe banana, peeled and sliced lengthwise
1 dash cinnamon
1/2 ounce banana liqueur
1 ounce white rum
1/2 ounce dark rum
1 large scoop vanilla ice cream

Melt brown sugar and butter in flat chafing dish. Add banana and sauté until tender. Sprinkle with cinnamon. Pour in banana liqueur and rum over all and flame. Baste with warm liquid until flame burns out. Serve immediately, putting ice cream on top.

PUTNAM KITCHENS
Dana Clarrissimeaux

Dana Clarrissimeaux, director of design for Putnam Kitchens, estimates that at least 75 percent of her clients are dual-working couples or families. Because they often do not have time to cook, many of her clients tend to use their kitchen more for entertaining than everyday meal preparation. "Today, kitchens are more than just a functional layout," she claims. "People want appeal along with practicality."

In the eighteen years that she has been in the business, Clarrissimeaux has also seen a shift in who is working in the kitchen. She theorizes that one of the reasons for the growth in the use of commercial cooking equipment in homes is that more men are preparing food. "Men tend to create more as they cook, and they like to do it on a grander scale," she comments. "Commercial equipment is perfect for that."

Clarrissimeaux says her favorite part of design is "taking the clients' dreams and making them happen." Their goal, asserts Dana, is to design environments rather than just kitchens.

Her own lifestyle is frenetic, so when she entertains for groups of friends in her cottage on the water, Clarrissimeaux likes to keep things as simple as possible. "If I get too involved with my cooking," she says, "I don't have time to be involved with my guests."

MEDITERRANEAN DRESSING FOR SPINACH SALAD
(Combine in blender)
1 large garlic clove crushed
1/2 teaspoon salt
1/2 teaspoon paprika and pepper
2 tablespoons tarragon vinegar
grated rind from one large lemon

Add Beating Slowly
1/2 cup olive oil
3 tablespoons sour cream

Chill for one hour minimum
Mix equal portions of fresh spinach and romaine lettuce. Add fresh large mushrooms sliced thin.
Garnish with crumbled bacon, extra crisp.

LaMantia Kitchen Design Studio: False drawer fronts filled with colorful candy add a uniquely charming aspect to an unpretentious space, while paying tribute to the family's candy-making business.
▲

REGENCY KITCHENS & CUSTOM INTERIORS
Rochelle Kalisch

"When you cook something for another person or a group of people, you infuse your spirit into what you prepare. There is a transference," says Rochelle Kalisch of Regency Kitchens. "I feel the same way about design." Kalisch brings a spiritual element into everything she does, whether it is designing kitchens, cooking, raising her five children or oil painting.

Kalisch's mother, who is Hungarian, taught her to make the veal stew with sweetbreads. Her family usually eats the meal on holidays. "Holiday time is great in our home," she remarks. "Everyone is in the kitchen preparing food and telling stories."

Since she and her husband Rueven work in the same hectic business, they value the time they spend preparing meals with their children. "When I design a kitchen for a family, I try to remind them of things they could do together that they may not have considered," Kalisch comments.

Her background in art is evident when Kalisch discusses her philosophy of kitchen design. "Designing a kitchen is an interactive experience," she says. "The space is not a still life, it is an element of expression."

Kalisch finds that working with her clients is in many ways a learning experience. "I see how people work together as a couple or family. Often, I play the role of peacemaker or listener," says Kalisch. "After working with people for months at a time, I have this huge family of friends."

MOM'S HUNGARIAN VEAL STEW WITH SWEETBREADS
2-1/2 pounds shoulder of veal
1 pound sweetbreads - preferably veal
2 tablespoons oil
1 medium onion, diced
1 garlic clove, minced
1 medium green pepper, cut into cubes
1 medium tomato, cut into wedges
1 teaspoon sweet paprika
freshly ground black pepper to taste
salt to taste

Cut veal into 1-1/2 inch cubes. Preboil sweetbreads; remove cartilage and skin. Sauté onions in oil until golden brown. Add meat and cook on low flame, covered, for 1/2 hour.

Add sweetbreads and spices. Sprinkle with paprika. Add green pepper and tomato. Add 1 cup of water and bring to a boil. Simmer for approximately 1 hour.

Serve over rice, potatoes or pasta. Garnish with parsley sprigs.

Rutt of New York City
George Rallis

George Rallis of Rutt of New York City remembers fishing with his father in the waters of the northern Aegean Sea near the Greek island of Lesvos, where he spent his childhood. "My father taught me to clean and cook fish," he says. "This squid recipe goes back a long time." Since his father was a chef in various restaurants, Rallis grew up watching him cook and tasting his creations.

Now, Rallis prepares calamari (squid) and fish with his eight-year-old son in his kitchen at home. "We get flour everywhere," laughs Rallis. "Usually I destroy the kitchen when I cook." Rallis and his wife usually split the cooking, but he is in charge of cooking any fish.

Rallis says that the secret of preparing the squid is to be sure it is undercooked. "The calamari should be cooked only two or three minutes," he explains. "The problem in restaurants is that they sometimes cook the fish five minutes, and then it comes out as hard as a shoe sole."

Since calamari is a delicacy, Rallis serves it for parties as a side dish or appetizer. He prefers to serve it with fish, but claims it could go with meat or poultry as well.

GREEK CALAMARI
A Mediterranean treat! Best when served hot with crusty bread, Greek salad and retsina or ouzo.

2 pounds calamari (squid)
2-3 cups extra virgin Greek olive oil
3/4 cup flour
lemons
salt and pepper to taste

The squid must be as fresh as possible. Wash the squid thoroughly, removing the rigid inner membrane. Retain the eggs. Carefully remove the casing of ink which is attached to the inside. Separate the head with the tentacles, as it will be fried whole.

Slice squid into 1/2-inch horizontal rings. Wash pieces again. Roll the pieces in flour and shake in a colander until they retain a very thin coating.

Olive oil should be heated in a large deep frying pan. Cook for 2 or 3 minutes if the squid is large. Drain on paper. Salt lightly. Drizzle with wedges of lemon.

LA Associates: A striking desk recessed into an arched wall provides ample space for organizing household activities.

▲

Rutt of New York City: A grape-and-vine motif visually lengthens the cabinets while adding exuberant color to the tile backsplash and island.

▲

St. Charles of New York
Bob and Karen Schwartz

Bob Schwartz and his wife Karen met while designing kitchens. Since then, they have designed three of their own kitchens together. According to Bob, "it must be in our blood." He says, "There have been times when we have been diametrically opposed to each other about the use of a space." The solution? "She always wins," he says quickly. Then he adds with a smile, "Actually, we usually reach a happy medium."

The Schwartz household is lively. The couple is raising four children ranging from a newborn to a thirteen-year-old; they entertain often; and they run a thriving business. Says Karen Schwartz, "I enjoy being busy. I am one of those people who works better at a faster pace."

"We spend inordinate amounts of time in the kitchen," adds Bob. "Our lifestyle dictates that we include everything from a cooking and entertaining area to a television to study areas in the kitchen."

According to Bob, "People today are doubling and tripling their budgets for the kitchen because a high quality kitchen equals a high quality of life."

"My favorite part of my work," he adds, "is when a client has seen a completed project and is elated that we have interpreted his or her thoughts and needs into something tangible. In effect, we have created something from nothing."

Karen Schwartz agrees. "The best kitchen," she says, "is the one that makes the client happy."

Shields & Company
Gail Shields-Miller

"Kitchens today have to be comfortable but practical," says Gail Shields-Miller. "I love the warmth of a traditional kitchen, but it must be contemporary in function."

Miller always cooks Italian food "because it is so simple." She serves her famous homemade manicotti buffet-style on New Year's Eve to a large group of guests.

Miller says that the dish reflects the more casual mood of today. "Food preparation is no longer an isolated, formal activity," she asserts. The kitchens in both her country and city home look out onto the adjoining living areas, allowing Miller to interact with her family or guests as she cooks.

"We love to entertain, but it is usually at the last minute and casual," says Miller. "We tend to cook more simply now." Miller adds that one of the secrets of her entertaining is to prepare part of the menu and buy the rest. "There is so much available today," she explains.

The Miller family usually cooks on weekends. "We are very 90-ish that way," laughs Miller. "We have three chefs in the family: my husband, my son and me."

LA Associates: Pots and pans are at the cook's fingertips thanks to a pair of deep drawers conveniently situated beneath the stove.

MANICOTTI CRÊPES WITH SPINACH AND CHEESE
yields about 24 stuffed crêpes
tomato sauce (recipe follows)
2 pounds fresh spinach, stems removed, or 1 box (10 ounces) frozen spinach,
thawed and squeezed dry
2 pounds whole-milk ricotta cheese
1/2 teaspoon freshly ground pepper
1/2 teaspoon salt
1/2 cup (4 ounces) freshly grated Parmesan cheese, plus more for serving
24 crêpes (recipe follows)
1 pound mozzarella, coarsely shredded

Lightly grease an 11x15x2 roasting pan. Pour 2 cups of the tomato sauce into
the pan and tilt to coat evenly. Set aside.

Bring a large pot of lightly salted water to a boil over high heat. Add half
the fresh spinach and stir until wilted. Remove to a colander with a slotted
spoon, drain and cool. Repeat with the remaining fresh spinach. When cool,
squeeze the spinach to remove as much moisture as possible. Chop the fresh
spinach or the frozen spinach leaves and transfer to a medium bowl. Add the
ricotta, pepper, salt and 1/2 cup of the Parmesan cheese; stir to blend well.
Set aside.

Preheat oven to 400 degrees. Lay out the crêpes on a large work surface.
Sprinkle 1-1/2 tablespoons of the shredded mozzarella over each crêpe,
leaving a 1-inch border around the rim.

Mound 2 tablespoons of the spinach and ricotta mixture in the center of
each crêpe. Fold the right side of the crêpe over the filling; then fold up the
bottom, fold down the top and fold the left side over to seal. Repeat with
the remaining crêpes. Arrange the filled crêpes, seam side down, in the
prepared pan.

Spoon 4 cups of tomato sauce over the crêpes. Cover loosely with foil. (The
recipe can be made to this point up to 1 month ahead and frozen.) Bake the
assembled dish for about 1 hour, or slightly longer if frozen, until piping hot.
Shortly before serving, reheat the remaining 2 cups of tomato sauce. Serve
the manicotti crêpes with more of the hot tomato sauce and lots of grated
Parmesan cheese on the side.

ZESTY TOMATO SAUCE
yields 2 quarts
3 tablespoons olive oil
1 large onion, chopped
2 large garlic cloves, minced
1 large red bell pepper, chopped
3 cans (35 ounces each) peeled Italian plum tomatoes
1-1/2 tablespoons minced fresh basil or 2 teaspoons dried
1 tablespoon minced fresh oregano or 1 teaspoon dried
1/2 teaspoon freshly ground black pepper
1/4 cup freshly grated Parmesan cheese
1/4 teaspoon salt

In a large nonreactive saucepan or small dutch oven, heat the oil over
moderate heat. Add the onion and cook, stirring, until translucent, about
5 minutes. Add the garlic and red bell pepper and cook, stirring, 5 minutes
longer. Add the tomatoes with their juice and crush lightly with a fork. Stir
in the basil and oregano. Bring just to a boil, reduce the heat to moderately
low and simmer, uncovered, for 2 hours, stirring occasionally.

Reduce the heat to low and stir in the black pepper and Parmesan and salt.
Simmer gently for 1 hour longer. (The sauce can be made and refrigerated up
to 2 days ahead or kept frozen up to one month.)

CRÊPES
yields about 24 crêpes
2 cups all-purpose flour
pinch of salt
6 eggs
3 cups milk
soft unsalted butter

In a large bowl, whisk together the flour and salt. In a medium bowl, beat the eggs. Gradually whisk in the milk until blended. Add the egg mixture to the flour in 3 batches, whisking until blended after each addition. Transfer the batter to a pitcher or a large measuring cup.

Heat a 6-inch crêpe pan or non-stick skillet over moderately high heat. Wipe the pan with buttered paper towels. Pour about 1/3 cup of the batter into the pan to thinly coat the bottom. Tilt and rotate the pan quickly to coat it evenly with batter. Cook until the edges are starting to brown, about 1 minute. Turn the crêpe over and cook until small brown spots appear on the underside, about 30 to 60 seconds more. Transfer the crêpe to a work surface and let cool. Repeat with the remaining batter.

On a baking sheet lined with wax paper, stack the cooled crêpes with more wax paper in between.

LaMantia Kitchen Design Studio: Casual comfort permeates every detail of this country kitchen.

▲

THURSTON, INC.
Steve MacDonald

Twenty years ago, Steve MacDonald left his job in St. Louis to move to the West Coast. On the way, he stopped to see a friend in Aspen, Colorado, and never left. In 1977, he founded Thurston, Inc., selling kitchen cabinets. Today, the company boasts nine offices throughout Colorado and 45 top designers.

"What makes our company work is people," says MacDonald. "I am still surprised at how close the designer and client become when they are serious about a project. The kitchen designer learns volumes about the client's lifestyle and family."

He adds, "In the kitchen, we aim to express the client's personality rather than the designer's. We always direct toward the end-user."

Of the 17 years he has been in business, MacDonald says, "It has been fun to participate in and watch the elevation of the kitchen and bath industry. The field is much more sophisticated today than when we began. Staying abreast of new technology and trends is challenging."

MacDonald chose to include his "drunken chicken" recipe as an example of a dish he and his wife enjoy sharing with friends on their gazebo in their beautiful backyard in Denver.

GRILLED CHICKEN
Wine: White/Italian Terre di tufo
4 boneless chicken breasts

Marinade:
1 cup tequila
3/4 cup Rose's lime juice
2 shallots finely chopped
6 minced garlic cloves

1/2 cup cilantro chopped
1/2 teaspoon oregano
1/2 teaspoon ground cumin
1/2 cup green taco sauce

Combine all ingredients. Marinade 4 boneless chicken breasts overnight.
    Grill chicken. Save marinade and drizzle over chicken when complete. Top with papaya salsa.

PAPAYA SALSA
2 papayas, peeled, seeded and chopped
1 red onion, peeled and chopped
1 red pepper, seeded and chopped
1 small jalapeno, seeded and minced
1 cup cilantro chopped

Mix together all ingredients.

COUSCOUS:
1 tablespoon olive oil, heated
3 shallots
chicken broth
12 ounces couscous
small box raisins

Add 3 shallots finely chopped, cook until slightly tender. Add chicken broth, bring to a boil, turn heat off and add the couscous with a small box of raisins. Cover and let sit for 10 minutes. Before serving, stir in 3 to 4 tablespoons of prepared pesto sauce.

**LaMantia Kitchen Design Studio:
Plate storage racks placed at eye
level offer creative opportunities
for incorporating dashes of color.**
▶

INDEX OF KITCHEN & BATH DESIGNERS

Index of Photographers